CONTEMPORARY SOUTHEAST ASIA

ROBERT C. BONE, Jr.

FLORIDA STATE UNIVERSITY

Random House, New York

For My Wife: Without whom, this or little else would ever have been possible.

First Printing
© Copyright, 1962, by Random House, Inc.
All rights reserved under International and Pan-American Copyright Conventions. Published in New York by Random House, Inc., and in Toronto, Canada, by Random House of Canada, Limited.
Library of Congress Catalog Card Number: 62-10675
Manufactured in the United States of America by
The Colonial Press Inc., Clinton, Mass.

Design by Jacqueline Schuman

CONTENTS

CONTEMPORARY SOUTHEAST ASIA

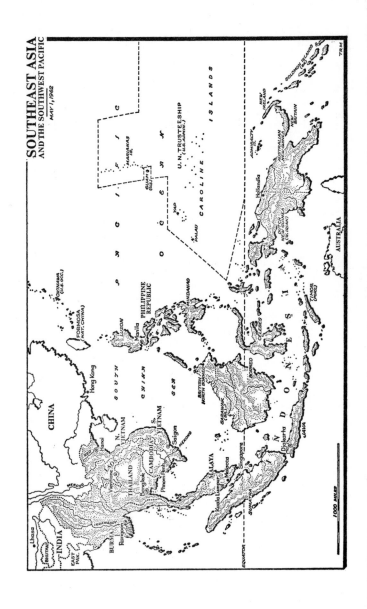

SOUTHEAST ASIA
AND THE SOUTHWEST PACIFIC
MAY 1, 1962

INTRODUCTORY SURVEY

Contemporary Southeast Asia is an exciting cultural complexity, a political fiction, and an international problem of uncertain but disturbing proportions. In all these categories the element of paradox and contradiction is dominant.

The term "Southeast Asia" came into general use during World War II as a matter of geopolitical convenience for military strategists. It was used, often without precise designation, to include the southeastern section of the Asian continent which lay between India and China. The term usually also included the thousands of islands north of Australia which stretch in a great arc from the tip of the Malay peninsula through the Philippines into the South China Sea.

As generally understood now, continental Southeast Asia begins in the west with Burma. Actually in climatic and geographical terms, east Pakistan also might be included except that its focus lies in its western section. Therefore, a somewhat arbitrary line for defining the western extent of continental Southeast Asia is drawn at the Burmese border. The giant peninsula that comprises the continental part of the area includes eight separate entities ranging in size from approximately 260,000 square miles each of Burma and Thailand to the 220 square miles of the city state of Singapore. Also included within continental Southeast Asia are the Federation of Malaya and the four parts into which the former French empire of Indo-China has been split since 1954—North and South Vietnam, Laos, and Cambodia. Population figures vary as widely as the areas of the countries involved, ranging from the approximately 22,000,000 inhabitants each of Burma and Thailand to the more than 1,500,000 swarming through the streets of Singapore.

Insular Southeast Asia swings in a great U-shaped arc from the western tip of the huge (167,000 square miles) island of Sumatra to Luzon, northernmost and largest (40,000 square miles) island of the Philippine archipelago. Most of insular Southeast Asia is contained within the myriad islands of the Indonesian archipelago and politically within the boundaries of Southeast Asia's shaky giant, the Republic of Indonesia. The other political entities are the Republic of the Philippines and the remaining colonial possessions in Southeast Asia. These comprise the three British areas of North Borneo, Sarawak, and Brunei, and yet another one of those fragments of empire to which Portugal clings so stubbornly, the eastern half of otherwise Indonesian Timor.

Southeast Asia's present population is anyone's guess, but most estimates place it at approximately 200,000,000. In spite of its phenomenal growth over the last 150 years, particularly over the last half century, from the estimated 10,000,000 of 1800, large areas of Southeast Asia are still virtually uninhabited. The deltas of the important river systems, such as the Red River of northern Vietnam, the Irrawaddy in Burma, the Menam Chao Phraya in Thailand, in contrast have population densities ranging as high as 1500 persons per square mile, the highest in the world for an agricultural area. A glance at a population map of the area reveals particularly heavy concentrations of population in the fertile plains of central Java—where on an island approximately the size of Louisiana some 55,000,000 people live, in southern Thailand, and in northern Vietnam. But equally striking are the vast underpopulated areas in continental Southeast Asia and, for example, on the huge island of Borneo (Kalimantan) in the Indonesian archipelago.

Physically and climatically, Southeast Asia has been described in a standard geographical reference work on the area as having a setting "of extremes of relief (deltaic plains and mountains) and a climate mostly approaching the wet limit for plant life but merging into monsoonal types." * Few areas so large have such climatic uniformity; the yearly temperatures throughout Southeast Asia vary but little from around a norm of 80 degrees Fahrenheit. Agricultural existence is conditioned by the wet and dry seasons with much of the area receiving as much as 80 inches of rainfall a year. Nor is the abundant rainfall, which makes Southeast Asia one of the great crop-producing areas of the world, the only way in which water has affected the destinies of the area.

In insular Southeast Asia geography has conspired to focus attention on the inner seas rather than on the Pacific. On both Java and Sumatra, for example, the coastal plains stretch from the western mountain ranges towards the Java Sea and the Straits of Malacca. In the formation of this great natural gateway between the Indian and the Pacific oceans, Nature destined Southeast Asia for an important geopolitical role from the time that shipping first became important. Great empires arose early here; and by the beginning of the Christian era, the Malaccan straits were already a well-travelled ocean highway, the control of which affected economic and political destinies far removed in space. As a sixteenth-century Portuguese pioneer in geopolitical thinking expressed it, "Whoever is lord of Malacca has his hand on the throat of Venice!"

Climate and geography, then, have combined in Southeast Asia to produce a potential treasure house of agricultural abundance for various peoples both isolated and linked by natural circumstances. From the beginning of time, Southeast Asia has attracted powerful outside interests; throughout history its people have known pressures from other cultures and political forces—traditionally In-

* Dobby, E. G., *Southeast Asia*. London, 1950, p. 282.

dian and Chinese, with the West becoming the dominant force in the seventeenth century. Japan briefly, in the political sense, supplanted traditional Chinese influence in the mid-twentieth century. It has well been said of Southeast Asia that "there is probably no other area of the world so richly endowed with diverse cultural strains and so prepared to view the world tolerantly." *

In population, as in cultures, Southeast Asia has acquired unique diversity over the centuries. The major ethnic basis of Southeast Asia's approximately 200,000,000 people stems from two great waves of migration, which took place some time between the second millennium and the sixth century B.C. These successive waves of peoples, known as the Proto- and the Deutero-Malays, pushed the original inhabitants into more remote areas—a process repeated so often that, as one distinguished anthropologist summarizes it, ". . . in this part of the world the range and variety of peoples and cultures are truly unmatched anywhere else on earth." † The Proto-Malay wave of invasion is still represented in Southeast Asia by such peoples as the Jakun of Malaya, the Bataks of Sumatra, and the majority of the Dayak peoples of Borneo. The Deutero-Malays, sometimes called the coastal Malays, are represented by the majority population of modern Malaya, the millions of Javanese of Indonesia, and the Sudanese and the Madurese peoples of that nation. Indeed, they are the dominant Malay type of Southeast Asia.

Three waves of immigration into Southeast Asia deserve mention because of the important historic and modern roles played by the peoples concerned. The first of these were the Viets, who founded the Annamese empire and who make up most of the population of the two modern Vietnams. Some time between 500 B.C. and 300 B.C., these peoples, probably originating somewhere in South China, pushed down the invasion gap of the coastal plain, extend-

* DuBois, Cora, *Social Forces in Southeast Asia.* Cambridge, 1959, p. 27.

† Linton, Ralph, *The Study of Man.* New York, 1945, p. 663.

ing themselves as far as modern Cochin China. Further west, about 600 A.D., the Burman peoples repeated the process, defeating and conquering peoples who now make up the minority groups of modern Burma. Much later, in approximately 1300 A.D., the Thai-Shan-Lao moved down the river valleys from their original homeland in the Kwantung-Yunnan plateau, occupying areas in eastern Burma and Laos as they went and defeating the Mons and the Khmers to lay the foundations of modern Thailand.

The result of these successive waves has been to create a patchwork quilt of racial and linguistic groups throughout the area. Modern Indonesia, for example, counts fifty-four distinguishable ethnic groups and over two hundred language groups. In such countries as Burma and Indonesia, the problem of minorities has been vexing and crucial, and has frequently been the cause of actual armed conflict. Modern Malaya, in a somewhat different sense, has also suffered from a serious minority problem. The minority group in this case is composed of the descendants of Chinese coolies brought in the nineteenth century to work the Malayan tin mines. Here, as elsewhere in Southeast Asia, the Chinese have displayed an amazing upward mobility, economically, and a fecundity that has swelled their numbers throughout Southeast Asia in general to approximately 12,000,000.

In both cultural and religious terms Southeast Asia presents a panorama of bewildering complexity. Within the area is such a great, twentieth-century city as Singapore, while a few hundred miles away are primitive peoples pursuing ways of life that have scarcely changed since the first Portuguese ship visited the area; indeed, the way of life of these primitive peoples is little different from what it was at the time of Christ. Also included in Southeast Asia are sophisticated civilizations whose ancestors were building such masterworks as Angkor Wat and Borobudur when western civilization was at the very nadir of its Dark Ages.

One of the most difficult problems confronting the student of Southeast Asian cultures is that of distinguishing between the indigenous and the imported. From the earliest times, as we have noted, the area has been a constant source of interest to outsiders by virtue of its geopolitical position and basic resources. The very beginnings of recorded history show strong and long-established Indian and Chinese influence. Aside from the Philippines which, because of its geographical location, was least touched by foreign impact until the European period, the remainder of Southeast Asia is usually divided into two areas of cultural influence. The smaller of these, where Chinese cultural influences are regarded as dominant, is comprised within the two Vietnams, consisting of Tonking, Annam, and Cochin China. It has been suggested that the mountainous spine which stretches down almost the whole length of the Indo-Chinese peninsula serves as a natural boundary between the Chinese-influenced areas and all the rest of Southeast Asia, which is generally assigned to the Indian sphere of cultural influence. This generalization is made in spite of the fact that for many centuries, while China was a strong and centralized monarchy, there never was an Indian equivalent. Chinese hegemony and tribute-collecting extended over wide areas of Southeast Asia for considerable periods of time. Yet, except for the areas included in modern North and South Vietnam, Chinese cultural and religious influence had little impact.

There is no agreement, even among the most distinguished authorities, as to why this was so. One of the most eminent American anthropologists (Ralph Linton) has suggested that the explanation may lie in the fact that Indian culture was more emotionally acceptable. More recently, another scholar well informed on Southeast Asia, Lucian Pye, has suggested the explanation that "Chinese culture was an integrated whole" while "in Southeast Asia, except where the Chinese directly imposed their own form of government, the necessary framework for an acceptance of Chinese culture was lacking."

Part of the explanation may well be that the Chinese appeal was intellectual, the Indian emotional. In the houses of both Hinduism and Buddhism there are so many rooms that prince or peasant, scholar or simpleton, can with equal ease find his spiritual home. The Indian religious appeal demands none of the supporting "infrastructure" that is required by the Chinese ethical concept, and that causes it to lack focus when removed from its indigenous background.

Whatever the explanation, it is fallacious to think in broad sweeping terms of "the Indian" or "the Chinese" areas of Southeast Asia; for the mass of the people, both then and now, have lived in terms of their own indigenous concepts and patterns. In Southeast Asia, as among other predominantly peasant peoples, the rhythm of agricultural existence and the powerful spiritual forces which personify the aspects of daily existence have led to an almost instinctive yet highly logical animism. Southeast Asia has been referred to as the "crossroads of religion." But a crossroads implies a passing-by and this has scarcely been the case in Southeast Asia; for here, over the long centuries, the impact of one religion has scarcely subsided before another has taken its place. The original animism, Hinduism, Buddhism, Islam, Confucianism in Vietnam, Christianity in widely-scattered areas, all have left their coloration. It is as though Southeast Asia were an often-varnished table on which coat after coat of different lacquers have been applied successively.

On the religious maps of the world, Malaya (50 per cent) and Indonesia (93 per cent) are colored as Islamic countries, Burma (82 per cent), Cambodia (95 per cent), Laos (90 per cent), and Thailand (94 per cent) are placed in the Buddhist column, and the Philippines (93 per cent) and Vietnam (95 per cent) are characterized respectively as being Christian and Buddhist-Confucianist. Although all these countries vary in religious allegiance, it seems safe to generalize that the average peasant is primarily an animist who thinks first of propitiating local deities and then of wider spiritual loyalties. Southeast Asia has seldom rejected a new religion, but has almost never completely surrendered to one. The catholicity of this religious assimilation is well illustrated, by the Cao-Dai sect of Vietnam with its almost ludicrous attempt to combine animism, Taoism,

Confucianism, Buddhism, Christianity, and the deification of Victor Hugo.

However uncertain the generalizations we can make about religious influences on Southeast Asia, we are on far more solid ground when we turn to the political sphere. The Chinese impact within its restricted area of influence, in terms of the dominance of Confucianism and a mandarinate, and the far wider Hindu and Buddhist influences on the political thinking and the evolution of the rest of Southeast Asia were so profound that they are still obvious.

In particular, the Hindu-Buddhist political-cosmological concepts furnished the basis on which the first great empires of Southeast Asia were established. Common to each of these was the existence of a governmental structure and a capital city which sought microcosmically to reproduce on earth the pattern in which the gods had arranged the heavens. At the center was the divine ruler who, to quote a title still used by the Susunan of Surakarta in Java, was "the divine nail from which the world hangs." Like medieval Europe it was a status civilization which provided a religious, ethical, and morally seamless web within which all life could be lived. Not the least of the results of the European period was the destruction or serious damaging of this cosmological-political world view. Instead of an adequate substitute, there was proffered the cold and lifeless apparatus of the western state, deliberately devoid of religious, emotional, and cosmological meaning.

The way in which nation after nation of Southeast Asia has felt it necessary, over the past decade, to re-examine and frequently to reshape the inherited state structure illustrates the failure of this structure to meet the political and cultural needs of the area. Nor even among the most acculturated of the governing elite of the new nations have "the old gods" been forgotten. Burma, it will be remembered, started its independent existence as a nation at the rather improbable hour of 3:40 A.M. because astrological omens had indicated that it was a propitious time and, striking as the differences of temperament and training are between U Nu of Burma and Sukarno of Indonesia, both consult their private astrologers before undertaking any important steps. In both the "Chinese" and the "Indian" areas of modern Southeast Asia, the magic powers of the unseen world play a hidden but important role in shaping the decisions of statesman and peasant alike.

As the distinguished anthropologist, Cora DuBois, has pointed out in her brief but classic study, *Social Forces in Southeast Asia,* from a very early period the native social structure of the area has been based on a class system sharply divided into the vast masses of the rural peasantry and the very small group of the aristocracy. The role of the aristocracy in western terms can perhaps best be equated with that played by the French nobility in the time of Louis XIV. Their whole world it will be remembered was the court of the great Sun King, and the Monarch himself the omniscient source and center of all power, privilege, and economic and social status.

In much the same fashion, the world outlook of the Southeast Asian aristocracy was centered on the microcosm of the divine cosmological order represented by the capital city and its god-king. Hierarchy, power, and privilege were its dominant concepts; intrigue, subtle plottings, and frequently murderous rivalries were its accepted ways of life. One of the most significant factors in the consolidation of European hegemony in Southeast Asia was the cynical and, on both sides, coldly calculated *mariage de convenance* between the indigenous aristocracy and the European interlopers. Very early in the game the Europeans learned the intricacies of court intrigue: they profited from the tolerance by the ruling elite of yet another set of foreigners at the cosmopolitan courts and from the aristocracy's desire not only to keep what it had but to increase its political and economic power. In Indonesia, in Indo-China, in Malaya, large sections of the native aristocracy chose to come to terms with the new and dynamic forces that were so irresistibly dominating their worlds. As in India, many members of the Southeast Asian aristocracy came to identify their interests wholeheartedly with those of the colonial power, which not only sustained but enhanced their privileged social and economic positions. It is easy for Westerners to forget that nationalism is a very recent concept anywhere in the world. One has only to recall, for example, that throughout the Hundred Years' War between France and England, an important section of French nobility supported the English side.

Just as the court dominated the life of the nobility, the village, in ancient Southeast Asia was and still is the focus of peasant existence. Centering on agriculture (almost always wet rice cultivation), peasant existence was regulated by complicated and elaborate personal relationships and customary law. Both rice cultivation and the other basic economic activity, fishing, demanded a high degree of communal activity. In addition to the god-king and the rituals of the state religion, the peasantry also worshiped local animistic deities, interpreted by priests and diviners, and the aid of ancestors could be implored. As with the nobility, there seems to have been frequent recourse to black magic. For centuries the peasants of Southeast Asia have continued to provide the docile and uncomplaining basis on which states and empires have been built. Except for fleeting, savage jacqueries and modern nationalist movements, political life in Southeast Asia has never involved more than a minute fraction of people, who have acted out their power struggle on the back of masses so absorbed in their own village life that they were scarcely conscious that it was taking place.

Aside from the sharing of a concept of universal order which harmoniously linked men and gods, there was some interchange between nobility and peasantry. Uniquely able and brilliant men of peasant stock might enter the ranks of the elite through fortunate circumstances. This was particularly true, of course, in times of chaotic change. The folklore of Southeast Asia is filled with "Horatio Alger" stories of bright young peasant boys whose native ability makes them the "prime ministers" or viziers of powerful rulers, carrying up with them their entire clan. The same precipitate upward mobility has occurred with beautiful peasant girls, although usually for reasons not directly connected either with intellectual brilliance or managerial ability.

In "Chinese" Southeast Asia (Vietnam), the mandarinate with its competitive examinations systematized the possibilities for such upward mobility, although obviously even the most brilliant son of a peasant was unlikely to be able to prepare for these gruelling examinations as easily or as well as a young man from a more privileged background. The reverse of this process of upward mobility took place to some extent in the indirectly governed colonial areas where those nobles who could not adjust to the new order retrogressed into the peasantry.

Southeast Asia's traditional social pattern does not seem to have produced any counterpart to that commercial middle class which, from the period of the late Middle Ages,* increasingly dominated European history. At the time of the initial European contacts, the Chinese and Indian merchant communities played important roles. Of the two, the Indian traders seem to have played a far more influential role in shaping the pattern of most of Southeast Asia's cultural and, probably, religious development. For reasons already mentioned, the Chinese remained far more a group apart than did the Indians; in the early period, and when mass migration occurred in the later colonial period, the Chinese were regarded, for good reasons, as an alien and predatory group by the native peoples. Functioning outside the social structure of native society, Chinese and Europeans served each other profitably. For example, the first great Governor-General of the Dutch East India Company on Java, Jan Pieterszoen Coen (1618-1623), pro-

---

* See the several essays written on "Asian Social and Economic History" by the brilliant Dutch scholar, J. C. van Leur, published in the collection entitled *Indonesian Trade and Society,* W. van Hoeve Ltd., The Hague/Bandung, 1955. Of particular interest is van Leur's essay "On Early Asian Trade," pp. 1-156. In another essay, "The World of Southeast Asia," in the same volume, van Leur suggests that the "Hinduization" of Southeast Asia was due less to colonization than to "the Indian hierocracy coming from the powerful Hindu states of southern India" as "scribal priests combining governmental skill and sacred legitimation." (p. 168)

phetically outlined the future economic symbiosis. In a policy memorandum he suggested that the most expeditious policy for the Company to follow was to limit its trade to that of a ". . . mighty wholesale dealer; the burghers (i.e. the Dutch merchants) should be active as middlemen, whereas retail trade should be left to the Chinese . . . who in this connection and even as merchants far exceed ours in ability . . ."

In the mature colonial period the Chinese, the Indians— particularly in Burma—and the Eurasians, who have been termed the "castaways of colonialism," together with the dominant European minorities, were important groups involved in, yet separate from, the already complex indigenous social structure. The destinies of all these groups, plus the never-assimilated original minorities, continue to be uncertain in the patchwork-quilt political divisions of contemporary Southeast Asia.

Especially in the political sphere it is impossible to speak in terms of "Southeast Asia." For Western Europe, one can speak of the prevalence of parliamentary democracy or, for the Soviet sphere, of the single-party state as a regional characteristic. For Southeast Asia no such generalization is remotely possible.

In technical constitutional terms Southeast Asia can be described, not very meaningfully, as containing nine independent nations, a city state with pre-World War I "dominion status," and four colonial areas. In terms of types of governments yet another basis of division can be used. Again, going by form rather than by content, the non-colonial areas of Southeast Asia could be divided into five republics, four monarchies, and a parliamentary-type city state with an elected head. But considering that the republics involved are as disparate as those of the Philippines, Indonesia, North and South Vietnam, and Burma, it is clear that there is wide variation indeed. For that matter, among the four monarchies, Malaya with its uniquely elected "paramount ruler" and its stable parliamentary democracy, Thailand with its government of and by a small political elite, Cambodia whose hereditary ruler functions far more as a twentieth-century one-party state leader, and the distraught little kingdom of Laos, there is bewildering complexity.

In political terms, in the twentieth century Southeast Asia has added a new dimension to its centuries-old role as an area where complex forces, originating far from the area itself, meet and clash. And, typically enough, new pressures and influences arise before the shock of those from the past is over. Southeast Asia had barely begun to assimilate the impact of late nineteenth-century western colonialism when it found itself faced with the problem of adjustment to what is perhaps the most revolutionary transformation in international affairs ever to take place. The concepts of political democracy, the startling possibilities of technological change, its political and economic implications, the shattering of the traditional cosmic concept, the intoxicating visions of independence and nationhood for all but Thailand were just beginning to be assimilated. Then came the precipitate collapse of western dominance during and after World War II. Southeast Asia was swept into the very center of a world in a state of frighteningly accelerating change where the oldest and most stable of nations were timid and uncertain. Technologically, before Southeast Asia had even begun to absorb the internal-combustion engine and electric power, it found itself confronted with the implications of jet travel and atomic energy. Politically, while the new nations were proudly acquiring all the paraphernalia of nineteenth-century nationalism from model constitutions to national anthems, the very globe itself had suddenly become the arena for a duel between super-powers.

Again in terms of new religions, history has repeated itself in twentieth-century Southeast Asia. Islam and Christianity in the sixteenth century had presented new and alternative choices virtually simultaneously in many areas. In the twentieth century the same was true of Marxism and, for want of a better term, Western Democracy. Both offered themselves as vehicles to express the nationalist revolutions; both were eagerly accepted by their adherents less in political than in religious terms; both were assayed for their ability to present a total cosmic picture which would serve in the twentieth century as a new basis for reintegration of severely shaken societies. Neither could find fulfillment in a narrow parochialism, for each ideology implied global allegiances. Both have avoided the inter-personal concepts of the old religions and think instead of whole societies and of the ultimate achievement of an economic and social order which would insure abundance and social justice.

Yet, and this is again a Southeast Asian characteristic, these ideologies have been at times deliberately reinter-preted in indigenous terms. Not only have they been reinterpreted, but in many respects, as with religious accre-tions in the past, curiously blended. Thus Sukarno of Indonesia can speak scathingly of western democracy while praising his own reworking of its basic concepts into a "guided democracy" more suited for his nation's needs. And Burma's U Nu could proclaim his country's ultimate socialist goals while conducting himself as a devout Bud-dhist and dealing warily with Moscow and Peking. The two extremes of adherence to the Marxist and Western world views are, of course, represented by North Vietnam and the Philippines. In the one case adherence was by conquest and suppression of opposition; the other is the instance of perhaps the world's most fortunate former colonial peoples. For the Philippines entered the cultural orbit of the west very early at a time when its peoples had everything to gain and little to lose. And, unlike the peoples of Africa who have had only one or two generations to leap from primitive society to the late twentieth century, the Philippines have had centuries.

In this initial section an effort has been made to suggest some of the forces which have played on Southeast Asia in the past, the fashion in which they have been assimilated and modified, and some of the complications this has created. Before turning to the historical development of Southeast Asia, the reader might like to refer to the Analytical Chart of Southeast Asian nations, which attempts to summarize some pertinent background data on contemporary problems.

ANALYTICAL CHART OF

Country	Area (sq. mi.)	Chief Exports	Population	Chief Minorities
BURMA	261,789	Teakwood Rice Cotton	20,457,000	Indians—1,000,000 Chinese—300,000 Mons, Shans, Arkanese, Karens—1,500,000
CAMBODIA	88,780	Forest Products Fish Rice	5,000,000	Vietnamese—350,000 Chinese—250,000 Chams—85,000
INDONESIA	735,865	Oil Tin Rubber Copra	90,000,000	Chinese—2,500,000 Europeans—50,000 Arabs—85,000
LAOS	89,000	Rice Maize Tobacco	2,000,000	Chinese—40,000 Viets—15,000
MALAYA	50,690	Rubber Tin	6,300,000	Chinese—2,300,000 Indians—700,000
PHILIPPINES	115,758	Copra Sugar Abaca	24,718,000	Chinese—270,000
SINGAPORE	217	(Commerce and Finance)	1,581,000	Malays—217,000 Indians and Pakistani—134,000
THAILAND	200,148	Rice Ore Rubber Timber	22,800,000	Malays—685,000 Chinese—2,360,000
VIETNAM, NORTH	62,000	Rice Coal	15,000,000	Thai-Meo—330,000 Tho-Nung—800,000
VIETNAM, SOUTH	65,000	Rice Rubber	13,000,000	Primitive Tribes—250,000 Chinese—800,000

SOUTHEAST ASIAN NATIONS

Religions	Degree of Literacy	Village Population	Governing Party (1962)	Official Form of Government	Dynamics of Political System
Buddhist—84% Islamic-Hindu—8% Christian—2%	60%	91%	The Army	Republic	Military Oligarchy
Buddhist—91%	20%	95%	Popular Socialist Party	Parliamentary Monarchy	Benevolent Authoritarian
Islamic—93% Christian—5% Buddhist—1.1% Hindu—2.7%	60%	80%	"National Front"	Presidential	Authoritarian Guided Democracy
Buddhist—90%	10%	98%	People's Party	Parliamentary Monarchy	Authoritarian Oligarchy
Islamic—50% Confucian-Taoist—39% Hindu—11%	40%	75%	Alliance Party	Parliamentary Monarchy (Elected King)	Competitive Democracy
Christian—93% Islamic—3.2% Pagans—1.5%	65%	75%	Nationalist Party	Presidential	Competitive Democracy
Confucian-Taoist—75%	65%	—	People's Action Party	Parliamentary	Competitive Democracy
Buddhist—95% Islamic—3%	20%	85%	(Military Dictatorship)	Constitutional Parliament	Competitive Oligarchy
Confucian-Taoist—95%	20%	90%	Worker's Party	Presidential Parliament	Totalitarian Dictatorship
Confucian-Taoist—85% Christian—8%	25%	88%	National Revolutionary Party	Presidential	Personal Dictatorship

THE HISTORICAL BACKGROUND
OF CONTEMPORARY
SOUTHEAST ASIA

1. *Until the Coming of the European*

History for contemporary Southeast Asia began when the Portuguese stormed Malacca in 1511. With the capture of this important trading center, a strategic economic-political position on the chief water route between the Indian Ocean and the Far East, the European era in Southeast Asia began. To say that this marks the beginning of "history" for modern Southeast Asia is not being "western-centric," for the capture of Malacca linked Southeast Asia meaningfully for the first time with the rest of the world, more importantly, with Western Europe. For the next four hundred years Western Europe exerted the influence that by the mid-twentieth century has remolded the other peoples of the earth in some variant of its own image. As the great British historian, Arnold Toynbee, has observed, many civilizations have waxed and waned, but the distinction of successfully impressing itself on other peoples as the global norm has been reserved to Western Europe.

It is also not possible to speak of "history" before the Portuguese came in the sense of meaningful change and evolutionary development. Myth and legend are generously intermixed with historical facts in the native chronicles; a good example of this is the famous Javanese historical epic of the fourteenth century, the *Nagarkertagama* of Prapanca; erudite Dutch scholars are still in violent disagreement over its proportions of myth and legend. For the centuries before the coming of the Portuguese, we can more or less accurately list the names of kings and trace the rise and fall of dynasties and empires, some of which, like the eighth-century Khmer dynasty of Cambodia or its Sailendra contemporaries in Java, left imposing architectural landmarks in the forms of great cities or monuments. The awe-inspiring Borobudur, for example, was built a good four centuries before the first stone was laid for Notre Dame.

But as far into the past as this mélange of myth, legend, and history goes, it has an unvarying element of cyclical repetition. The economic basis on which the great empires rise and fall remains unchanged. So does the role of the ruler, whether, in Hindu terms, he is considered the incarnation or descendant of a god or, in the Hinayana Buddhist concept, as the god's representative because he occupies the sacred palace. But in spite of the glaring contrast between the cosmological political structure of pre-European Southeast Asia and the determinedly secular basis of most of its governments today, there are intriguing points of similarity.

First of all, there is the fact that, in the past as in the present, the model for state organization in Southeast Asia came from outside the area; it was not a produce of indigenous growth. Cultural assimilation was never quite consummated, with the result that social integration remains incomplete. In the past as in the present, this produced alienation between elite and mass. The results were that the elite were culturally indoctrinated in the concept of authoritarian rule and decision-making but not with the need to consider any group except their own, and the vast majority of the population lacked any concept of government beyond the village level.

The second "modern" characteristic of the classic Southeast Asian political structure was its instability. Institutionally, governmental structure was rootless; there

was neither identification nor other emotional significance
for the masses. The closed and complete world of the
village was indifferent to, even if it knew, what particular
individual or family was the sacred symbol of the miniature cosmos of the state. And this cultural isolation was
intensified by the peculiar nature of the religious sanctions
which the kingship enjoyed; by his very deification the ruler
was removed from all effective restraints from any source
—except those of the assassin's knife or the poisoner's cup.
As with the later Roman emperors, every social and
cultural influence encouraged the exercise of total and un-
bridled power and self-gratification. (It is a realistic com-
mentary on mankind that in the history of despotic power,
Marcus Aurelius and Ashoka stand out in lonely gran-
deur!) The result was to make any current ruler not only
sacerdotally remote but frequently a prime target for
violent removal. Although his successor could drape himself in the same divine sanctions, the lack of any reg-
ularized procedure for the choice of that successor was an
invitation to violence and chaos. As a distinguished Aus-
trian anthropologist, Dr. Robert Heine-Geldern, has summarized it, "Under these circumstances it is no wonder
that the empires of Southeast Asia from the very beginning
were torn by frequent rebellion, often resulting in the
overthrow of kings or even dynasties." Schism in the social
body and an unstable atmosphere of political tension have
long been Southeast Asia's heritage.

The coming of Islam, like that of Christianity, falls
within the modern period. By the end of the thirteenth
century, Islam was already well established in various
seaport towns of northeastern Sumatra. Marco Polo found
many Moslems present in Perlak, situated in present-day
Atjeh, when he visited there in 1292; the first Moslem ruler
of the neighboring seaport of Pasai died in 1297. It was no
accident that Islam initially appeared in these seaports,
which were the first to be visited on the trading route
from South India. As is thought to have been the case with
both Hinduism and Buddhism previously, Indian merchants trading between India and the Southeast Asian

ports were the carriers of the new faith. Again, as before, Islam seems to have spread by official fiat. Various local rulers along the Straits of Malacca and the coast of northeast Java adopted it for reasons of their personal convenience. Probably the motivating factors were a mixture of honest conversion and the impressive material benefits which its adherents, as exemplified by the Bengali and Gujerati merchants, seemed to enjoy. Again in the traditional Southeast Asian pattern, the personal choice of the ruler, officially at least, determined the religious destiny of his people. Significantly Islam spread, if but slowly, in precisely those areas of Southeast Asia that had the most active trade contacts—the Malayan peninsula and the Indonesian archipelago. Although in large areas it was received as simply another coat of varnish, it is probable that in Southeast Asia as in India, Islam offered a welcome escape into a casteless religious egalitarianism.

It spread gradually through the Indonesian archipelago and into the southern Philippines, where its further progress was stopped by the crusading and ruthless counterattacks of the Spanish friars. It is worth noting that Islam's acceptance here was voluntary. It was both the last of the great Asian religions to enter Southeast Asia and also the last religious import to be substantially remolded by indigenous influences. Islam on Java, for example, largely tended to make a tolerant, eclectic adjustment to the old belief patterns. Moslem Sultans and Hindu Rajahs, very much as in India, engaged in shifting patterns of alliance and hostility. It remained for the European invaders to use religion as a touchstone of political reliability and forcible conversion as a weapon of conquest.

The European "discovery" of Southeast Asia in the sixteenth century was, of course, actually anything but that. As early as 150 A.D. the famous world map of Ptolemy depicted (not too inaccurately) India and "India beyond the Ganges" as areas already well and long known. Trade contacts with Southeast Asia went far back into history. The quest on which the European, above all the Portuguese, voyagers embarked in the late Middle Ages was to establish direct commercial contact with the treasure houses of Asia. They sought to eliminate the long chain of middlemen through whom the products finally reached Western Europe and thus acquire control of this fantastically profitable trade. And the Portuguese and the Spanish, who had waged seven centuries of war against Islamic invaders, still had a considerable amount of the crusading zeal which had worn itself out in the rest of Europe.

For a long time the opening of direct contact was simply beyond the technical capacities of the European explorers. It required almost a full century of slow and torturous voyages down the African coast before Vasco da Gama turned the Cape of Good Hope in 1487 and initiated that period of European dominance in Asia which one distinguished Indian diplomat-historian (K. M. Panikkar) has characterized as the "Vasco da Gama era." For Southeast Asia, as we have suggested earlier, it began with the Portuguese capture of the important trading center of Malacca in 1511. Apparently founded near the end of the fourteenth century, Malacca by the mid-fifteenth had become an important commercial center and, because of the conversion of its ruling prince, a source of Islamic influence.

Shortly before the arrival of the Portuguese, Southeast Asia had entered into one of those characteristic "power vacuum" phases when no great power exercised effective hegemony and the international relations of the area were uneasy and frequently explosive. In the Indonesian archipelago, the last great Hindu-Javanese thalassocratic empire, that of Majapahit, reached its apogee in the mid-fourteenth century and had been reduced by 1500 to a moldering remnant in east Java, no longer exercising either naval or commercial domination over the Indonesian and Malayan area. By the same time, Ming China, which a century earlier had driven out its Mongol overlords, had retreated into a policy of exclusive isolationism, following a brief period of imperial expansion in the early fifteenth century. Even Vietnam, the most traditionally vassal state, had regained its independence in the 1430's.

At the beginning of the sixteenth century there was no power in Southeast Asia capable of excluding the Europeans from the area in the sense that Imperial China or the Japanese Shogunate could bar contact with their territories. The Europeans were numerically very weak and not particularly technologically superior. So it was a uniquely fortunate circumstance that they arrived in the area during this period of extensive Balkanization. Malacca, although dominant in the area of the straits, was at most a city state. With the collapse of Majapahit, a series of little harbor principalities had sprung up along the northern coasts of Sumatra and Java. Further east, in the archipelago where lay the fabled Spice Islands, one of the major goals of European voyaging, the existence of numerous little antagonistic island principalities was to afford a notable opportunity for European intervention. This is best illustrated by the struggle between the miniature island-empires of Ternate and Tidore in the Moluccas. They were seized with alacrity first by the Portuguese, then the Spanish, then by the English, and finally by the Dutch East India Company.

Nor was mainland Southeast Asia any more unified. In the west, Burma as a political entity did not yet exist. In the north was the independent Shan area; in the center, the remnant of the old pagan kingdom; in addition, there were two other Burman kingdoms plus the Mon state of Pegu. Siam, soon to be involved in a hundred years' war with Burma, was little more united at the opening of the sixteenth century. A state of hostility had long existed between the Thai kingdom of Chiengmai in the upper Menam valley area and the southern Siamese kingdom of Ayuthia. In the area that would later become French Indo-China, the Khmers of Cambodia were engaged in constant war against Ayuthia. Vietnam, which in the late fifteenth century had expanded down the peninsula to absorb the ancient kingdom of Champa, had entered on a phase of dynastic degeneration in the early years of the sixteenth century: assassination became an almost routine method of imperial succession. Further, by 1545 the nation was plunged into a devastating dynastic civil war which lasted for most of the rest of the century. Seldom had Southeast Asia been more open to exploitation and penetration. In spite of this, the Europeans for several centuries, in contrast to the myth that they sprang like hungry wolves on their helpless victims, exhibited a timid, almost grudging, reluctance to assume the burdens of empire. The Spanish aside, the European groups asked no more than advantageous and protected trade connections.

2. The First European Phase, 1511-1869

In a scholarly and highly readable study, an English historian, Brian Harrison,* has suggested that in the sequence of "voyage, factory, fortress," the Portuguese "laid down the pattern of future European rule in Asia." It would seem appropriate, however, while still maintaining these single designations, to extend this classification one step further and add the term "colony" as the final development. Starting then from Mr. Harrison's stimulating three-word classification, it would seem that the European period in Southeast Asia might be outlined in terms of the following phases:

I. The "Voyage" Phase, 1509-1596;
II. The "Factory-Fort" Phase, 1511-1743;
III. Commercial Colonialism, 1743-1870;
    a. Private Empire, 1743-1800;
    b. Quiescence and Stalemate, 1800-1830;
    c. Political and Economic Transition, 1830-1870.
IV. The Phase of Imperial Colonialism, 1870-1957;
    a. The Indian Summer of European Rule, 1870-1905;
    b. The Gathering Storm Clouds, 1905-1941;
    c. Catastrophe and Liquidation, 1941-1957.

* Harrison, Brian, *South-East Asia, A Short History*. London, 1954.

Before discussing the four centuries in terms of these headings, some general comment on the major divisions is in order. It will be noted that phases I and II not only begin and end with seemingly arbitrary dates but also overlap and that phase II telescopes together the second and third of Mr. Harrison's descriptive terms. Although other students of Southeast Asia might disagree with the dates chosen, this method of procedure is no matter of arbitrary choice.

The initial "Voyage" phase includes the period of European probing into the Southeast Asian area when the initial establishment of contacts was still under way. The beginning of this phase is the date when the first Portuguese squadron appeared in the harbor of Malacca, two years before its capture. In 1596 the first Dutch ship dropped anchor in the busy northwest Java port of Bantam. Thus ended the initial phase of probing into Southeast Asia by the two European powers who were to influence its destiny most in the century ahead.

But already, long before the "Voyage" phase had been completed, the "Factory-Fort" phase had been initiated by the Portuguese capture of Malacca in 1511. It seems appropriate to link these as one; for, often, as in the case of Malacca, the establishment of a trading center ("factory") was accompanied by the erection of a fort for its protection. In other instances, as in Burma and Siam, for example, a local administration existed that could maintain order and take effective measures against any attempt to establish a military outpost. In these cases, the "fort" aspect of this phase remained unfulfilled. In areas such as India in the late Mogul period, what had begun as purely "factory" enterprises became "fort" as local authority grew feeble and measures for self-protection became urgent. The date 1743 seems appropriate to mark the close of this phase and the beginning of the next. For it marks the transition of the Dutch East India Company from its "factory-fort" phase into a new role as overlord of Java. As of this date, the last inheritor of the ancient Javanese imperial tradition, the lately developed (early seventeenth century) Islamic empire of Mataram became a landlocked dependency of the Company. Like its British counterpart in India during the same period, the company henceforth found itself forced further and further down the path of outright rule and acquisition of colonial possessions.

Unlike the Portuguese and especially the Spanish, there was little zeal on the part of either Dutch or English for the building of empire or the conversion of the heathen. For the sober-minded Calvinist merchants in Amsterdam and London regarded such wild romanticism as among the temptations of the devil. To the frustration of such aspiring empire-builders as Jan Pieterszoen Coen or Stamford Raffles, the "Gentlemen Seventeen" of Amsterdam and their London counterparts, the directors of the British East India Company, stubbornly and stolidly refused to think beyond the pleasant financial picture they hoped the next annual balance sheet would afford. (The remarkable achievement of the Dutch East India Company, which paid an annual 18 per cent dividend during the whole period of its existence between 1602 and 1800, is bound to stir envy in the most efficient modern board of directors.)

In terms of Southeast Asia this meant that, once the Portuguese had been displaced and the Spanish effectively restricted to the Philippines, for almost two hundred years there was only a European commercial policy in the area. There were many political *actions* taken by European interests, of course; but during this period there was no political *policy* as such. Such political actions as the European interests took were akin to those of the property owner who grudgingly buys the next lot to exclude undesirable neighbors.

It is indulgence in hyperbole to speak of a European "impact" on Southeast Asia during this period. The chief role played by the Europeans during this period was to interpose controls over the relations between Southeast Asia's chief productive centers and the rest of the world. The only Southeast Asians exposed to any close contact with the Europeans, and this merely peripherally and in

varying degrees, was the elite group of the ruling aristocracy. In relatively unified countries off the regular paths
of commercial activity, such as Burma or Thailand or the
sultanates of Malaya, even the state was little affected by
European "influence." For that matter, contact remained
superficial and businesslike even on Java where the Dutch
East India Company had set the policy, which would later
be followed by the Netherlands government, of virtually
incorporating the entire bureaucratic structure of the
Javanese aristocracy into its services. If nothing else, the
limited numbers of Europeans on Java would have made
effective cultural influence difficult, even if desired. It has
been estimated that, at the end of the eighteenth century,
Batavia (modern Djakarta), which possessed one of the
greatest concentrations of Europeans in all of Southeast
Asia, had a Dutch population, virtually all male, of less
than 300 out of its total population of around 12,000. (In
1815, Sir Thomas Stamford Raffles estimated Batavia's
total population at 47,217, of which 11,854 were Chinese
and only 543, Europeans.) One of the characteristics of
European contact with Southeast Asia until the opening of
the Suez Canal in 1869 was the very limited numbers of
persons involved, again mostly male.

For more than a century after the era of commercial
colonialism began in 1743, extensive areas of Southeast
Asia experienced but little European contact, let alone influence. Had Portugal and Spain remained on the world
scene as important powers, the situation might have been
quite otherwise; for both were imbued with a sense of
mission which quite transcended any solely commercial
motives. In terms of the three "G's" of the early European
adventurers, gold, God, and glory, the Portuguese, while
avid in the pursuit of the first of these categories, regarded
the second as almost equally important and were not un-
mindful of the third. But by mid-seventeenth century the
herculean effort which this tiny nation had made in
stretching its rule halfway round the world had brought
about a state of physical and moral collapse which reduced

Portugal's once extensive eastern empire to a portion of the small island of Timor in the Moluccan archipelago—a possession still held by Portugal today.

While the Spanish were quite ready to take over any treasure troves they came across, this was almost incidental to their pursuit of God and glory. In 1565 they established the first permanent European settlement in Southeast Asia on the island of Cebu and in 1571 founded the city of Manila. Aside from some abortive and feeble attempts at expansion in the Moluccas, promptly repulsed by the Dutch, the Spanish thereafter confined themselves to the geographically isolated Philippines. We have already noted that the Philippines were unique in being the one major area in Southeast Asia whose people had achieved no substantial degree of political unity and had not advanced culturally nor religiously much beyond the primitive level. Geography had isolated the various peoples of the islands from both Hindu and Buddhist influence; at the time the Spanish appeared, Islam had just begun to get a foothold in the southernmost part of the archipelago.

If the Spanish had had the Dutch or the English single-minded concentration on commerce, the Philippines would probably be numbered among the Islamic nations of the world today. But from beginning to end of their rule, the Spanish showed an indifference to commercial activity. That Manila became an important port on the Far Eastern trade routes was due largely to Chinese enterprise. Uniquely, in terms of a European colony, the Chinese in the Philippines found themselves in what amounted to the classic Southeast Asian situation before the Vasco da Gama era since neither the Spanish ruling group nor the masses of the native population were commercially oriented. The result was that with far less effort than it took in either the Dutch or the British areas, the Chinese found the way open to commercial success and rapid progress in economic status. The extent of government-sponsored commercial activity was confined to the single annual voyage of the "Manila galleon" which usually plied between the Philippines and Mexico, although sometimes directly to Spain.

Imbued with that same sense of conquering, proselytizing, and colonizing that they had shown in Latin America, the Spanish rapidly fanned out from Manila through the rest of the archipelago with the missionary friar as important a member of any expedition as the military commander. Except in the Islamic areas of the southern islands, where Spain never was able to bring the warlike "Moros" under control, the friars had little difficulty in converting the native population from its primitive animism. The result was that at a very early date, although as elsewhere various old beliefs and practices survived, the Philippines had become as uniquely Christian an area (93 per cent) in Southeast Asia as the island of Ambon in Indonesia. At an early date Ambon had fallen under intensive Portuguese and then Dutch influences, and to this day it is Christian in overwhelmingly (93 per cent) Islamic Indonesia.

As in Latin America, the Spaniards proceeded to create a New Spain. (Modern scholars find that a background knowledge of Latin America and its characteristic problems often offers a far better basis with which to begin studying the Philippines than to approach them from a Southeast Asian background.) Economically, Spain organized the Philippines on the basis of feudal tenure. The privileged native chieftain (datu) class was taken into partnership on a basis which, after a modern land-title system had been adopted in the nineteenth century, brought about the Latin-American situation of a small class of wealthy landowners controlling most of the arable land. The peasant population was virtually reduced to a peon (tao) level. In particular, during the nineteenth century the increasing introduction of a money economy led the small cultivator into debt, often to Chinese moneylenders. This accentuated the process of concentrated land ownership. "Land for the landless" was as meaningful a cry for the Luzon tao of the 1950's as it had been for the Mexican peon of the early 1900's.

The position of the mixed bloods in the Philippines was also very much in the Latin-American pattern during the period of Spanish rule. Everywhere else in Southeast Asia the mixed-bloods, the Eurasians, were a rather pathetic people apart, belonging neither to the indigenous nor to the European worlds, trusted by neither, patronizingly used by the Europeans, shunned by the natives. In the Philippines, the mestizos ranked in the social scale very much as they did in Spanish Mexico. They were below the small and overwhelmingly male, pure Spanish community. But they frequently bore distinguished names and came from families of wealthy landowners who regarded the peasant masses with the same contempt as the Spanish did. This group, as in Latin America, which could afford higher education at Manila's College of St. Thomas (which had become Southeast Asia's first university as early as 1645) and study and travel in Europe, provided the nucleus for the revolutionary elite which led the independence struggle. (José Rizal y Mercado, the martyred hero of Philippine independence, reportedly had both Chinese and Spanish ancestors "although his prevailing ancestry was Malay and contained both Tagalog and Ilocano strains." *) If true, this was an almost mystically symbolic mingling!

In administration also, the Spanish-American pattern was followed. At the time of the Spanish conquest, the peoples of the Philippines were organized on a village (*barrio*) basis with the family clan (*barangay*) as the basis of organization. Under Spanish rule, the barangay was transformed into a territorial unit; and a centralized administrative system was organized, going up through municipalities, districts, and provinces to the all-powerful governor-general in Manila.

Again, in typical Spanish-American fashion, the governor-general found himself engaged in a constant struggle for political hegemony with the archibishop, who was technically his subordinate. Besides being a political power, the Church became the greatest single landowner in the

* Forbes, W. Cameron, *The Philippine Islands* (Boston and New York, 1928), I, 52.

Philippines; the "friar lands" have been one of the thorniest problems in social politics with which the modern Philippines has had to deal.

Although, as no other people in Southeast Asia, the Filipinos were exposed to an intensive process of Europeanization and direct rule at a time when they were uniquely receptive culturally and socially, there was a curious fairy-tale quality about the long years of Spanish rule. It was almost as though, as in the case of Spain itself, life continued in terms of the social and intellectual patterns of the late Middle Ages. While this trance-like state of suspended evolution has a pleasant lotus-land quality about it as long as it endures, both Spanish and Philippine history seem to indicate that the awakening is likely to be brutal and traumatic.

The Philippines is unique not only in that its struggle for independence began decades before that of any other colonial area in Southeast Asia, but that its leadership, again in the Latin American pattern, was drawn predominantly from the mixed-blood group, which elsewhere in Southeast Asia when the independence struggles came was to show itself *plus royaliste que le roi* in its loyalty to the colonial systems. Although the first abortive revolt against Spanish rule occurred in 1872, it was not until twenty-four years later that the sustained effort to achieve independence by armed revolt began, under the leadership of Emilio Aguinaldo. It is interesting to note that the first of Southeast Asia's independence struggles was one of the last in the world to draw its inspiration completely from the concepts of the Revolution of 1789 rather than, as would be the case in the rest of Southeast Asia half a century later, from a curiously disparate mingling of the objectives of the revolutions of 1789 and 1917. Here, as in so many other respects, the Philippines has pursued a path separate from the other countries with which it is geographically linked. Nor was this apartness changed by the curious course of events which, after the initial failure of the Aguinaldo revolt, made the Philippines the one venture into imperial rule ever undertaken by the United States. Again, as in the case of the Spanish experience, the result would be to leave upon the Filipinos a psychological and cultural imprint different from that received by any other of the Southeast Asian peoples.

The Philippines aside, no other area of Southeast Asia experienced more sustained European contact and domination than did the Indonesian archipelago. Yet it would be difficult to find more contrasting situations: in the Philippines in the period between the founding of Manila in 1571 and the transfer to the United States in 1898 and in the Indonesian archipelago between the establishment of the hegemony of the Dutch Company over Java in 1743 and the beginnings of the liberal colonial period in 1870.

The Dutch period in Southeast Asia runs approximately from the mid-seventeenth century to the beginning of the nineteenth. While other European interests came and went during this time, only the Dutch stayed put throughout and methodically consolidated their position. The English East India Company maintained a small foothold in the Indonesian archipelago at Bencoolen, the pepper port of southwest Sumatra. Various efforts to expand elsewhere, notably on Borneo, proved unsuccessful. It was not until 1784 that Great Britain was able to break the Dutch monopoly in this area. The treaty of peace which ended the Fourth (and last) Anglo-Dutch War (1780-1784) gave reluctant but formal acknowledgment of the right of Great Britain to trade freely throughout the Indonesian archipelago. In 1786, Francis Light, a merchant of the India Company, concluded an agreement with the Sultan of Kedah which granted the right to occupy the island of Penang off the west coast of Malaya. Although the hopes of making Penang a second Malacca which would be able to supplant Batavia as the chief *entrepôt* for Southeast Asia were never realized, this was the modest beginning of Great Britain's role as an important colonial power in Southeast Asia.

Remoteness from the main trade routes and internal anarchy and foreign wars tended to make Burma, Thailand, and Vietnam dubious prospects for European commercial activity. In Burma, savage struggles between the Burmans and the minority groups, notably the Mons, discouraged commercial intercourse. By the mid-eighteenth century, Alaungpaya, founder of the last Burmese dynasty, had barely succeeded in finally uniting the country before he launched a bitter war against Thailand, which left both nations exhausted and neither victorious. Thailand, which had known civil war in the latter part of the seventeenth century, acquired its present ruling dynasty in the course of the war. After the sacking and almost total destruction of the traditional capital of Ayuthia by the Burmans in 1767, the crucial decision was taken to build a new capital at Bangkok, located near the sea. The result, in contrast to the deliberately chosen policy of self-isolation of Burma's rulers, was to make Thailand's monarchs and ruling elite far more accessible and amenable to western influences during that crucial period of the late nineteenth century when European empire building was at its peak. Like the Japanese, the Thais were to demonstrate a sure instinct for survival which would preserve their national independence.

Although in Vietnam French priests had begun missionary activity in the same year the Pilgrims landed on Plymouth Rock, geographical isolation and lack of trade incentive removed the Indo-Chinese peninsula from the focus of European interest until more than two centuries later. In the late eighteenth century, the victor in a dynastic struggle for the imperial throne did grant France the port of Tourane and the island of Condore off Cochin China in gratitude for the military assistance from French India which a French bishop had obtained. But this agreement of 1787 was forgotten in the cataclysmic events of 1789. It was another seventy years before France turned again to empire building in Indo-China.

Except in the Moluccas where the smallness of the areas and the sparseness of their population made the task easy, the Dutch East India Company, until its final bankruptcy in 1799, dedicated itself to the pursuit of a commercial policy, taking political actions only as a subsidiary and reluctantly used means to the end. As one of the most distinguished scholars of colonial development, J. S. Furnivall, summarizes it, ". . . ordinarily so long as the regents complied with Dutch requirements for supplies they were left to rule their subjects as they liked, strong in the support of the Company if their high-handedness should cause unrest." *

Before the end of the seventeenth century, the Company had already initiated that process of the reshaping of native economy which by the mid-twentieth century would be an important factor in the economic vulnerability and political instability of the new nations of Southeast Asia. Both the areas under direct Company control and those indirectly ruled were required to deliver fixed amounts of marketable produce at fixed prices to the Company's warehouses. The west Java sultanate of Bantam, abolished in 1813, was required to deliver a fixed amount of pepper, depending on the current European market conditions; the native regents of Mataram and Madura were held responsible for rice deliveries. In the course of the eighteenth century, coffee, indigo, and sugar, the production of which became a uniquely Chinese enterprise, were added to the list. In the Moluccas, the system of forced deliveries (*leveringen*) was applied even more stringently in the small islands over which the Company exercised direct rule in the production of cloves and other spices, although by the end of the eighteenth century the products of the once-fabulous Spice Islands had ceased to be important; coffee, sugar, and indigo from Java, along with camphor and cutch from the Outer Islands, had become the important export items.

Although direct political control was usually not present, the strict regulation of agricultural production plus forced labor obligations had direct and unfortunate influence on economic and social development in Java. As in India under the British East India Company, native industry and enterprise were ruthlessly circumscribed and sup-

* Furnivall, J. S., *Netherlands India: A Study of Plural Economy*. Cambridge, 1944, pp. 34-35.

pressed. All Java was made into one vast market garden for the production of export crops. The orderly rhythm of village economy was disrupted by the forced production requirements which, based as they were on the fluctuations of the export market, resulted in certain crops being destroyed in the fields one year and their being produced on unsuitable land in order to increase the year's yield in the next.

Even though Dutch practice did not permit the creation of huge private estates, as in the Philippines under Spanish rule, the effects of Dutch practice, nevertheless, drastically distorted the social relationships within indigenous society. As wide as the traditional gap between the peasant masses and the ruling elite had always been, the relationship had always rested upon and had been regulated by a large element of custom and consent. Even the most avaricious of rulers was aware that there was a point beyond which he dare not press for fear of alienating all elements of support from his own people. But with Dutch power behind him, this restraint was removed; and the alienation between elite and mass further increased. Nor was Dutch policy without psychological effect on the peasant masses. Systematically the Company reduced the prices paid the cultivator, resorted to forced labor, and alternated between enforced cultivation and enforced destruction of crops. The result was to remove all elements of incentive and to create a completely controlled environment quite outside the operation of the normal economic laws either of incentive or of supply and demand.

It was during the eighteenth century that the Chinese firmly consolidated that economic power which has become such an explosive political problem in modern Indonesia. They had fulfilled the middleman role which the Company had envisaged for them with such zealous efficiency that by the middle of the eighteenth century their wealth and power were sources of alarm to the Dutch authorities. In spite of a general massacre of the Batavia Chinese in 1740, induced by fears of a mythical uprising, they increasingly became the linking element in the whole economic structure. Like the Jews of Europe, their role was to be indispensable but hated, and always they were the inevitable scapegoats in times of social tension.

Also, in the course of the eighteenth century in East India Company Java, the form of what has been termed the "plural society" came into being. Its component parts were the Dutch, the Chinese, and the "native" worlds. In economic terms, they functioned like cog-wheels, the teeth of which intersect as much as necessary but no more. Other than that, it was as though the peoples concerned lived in separate worlds, each with its own standards of value and importance. Although first appearing in eighteenth-century Java, the plural society concept was to become the standard model for the organization of other colonial societies as they developed in the course of the nineteenth century. Neither in its heyday nor its legacy was it a happy or a constructive solution to the economic and social problems created by an ethnically and culturally polyglot society.

From the collapse of the Dutch East India Company into bankruptcy in 1799 to the establishment of the famous (or infamous) "Culture System" (*cultuur stelsel*) on Java in 1830 there was little change in the Southeast Asian scene. For half of this period the European powers were engaged in the death struggle of the Napoleonic wars. The most notable result of this for Southeast Asia was the five-year occupation of Java by the British during the period that the Netherlands was part of the French Empire. The British occupation is notable for the personality of the man who headed the British administration during this period; next to the first great governor-general of the Company, Jan Pieterszoen Coen, no single individual has played a more important role in the development of Indonesia and of all Southeast Asia than Sir Thomas Stamford Raffles.

During five hectic years, Raffles gave the creaking machinery of Dutch administration in Java the first overhaul it had had for almost two centuries. Summarizing the important transition point it marked in the colonial development of all Southeast Asia, Harrison comments, "Raffles's policy in Java may be regarded as a kind of preview of nineteenth-century liberal colonial policy in so far as it was formed of a mixture of humanitarian theory, realistic practice, and an oversimplified view of the problems and techniques of reform." * The Raffles period on Java was the inspiration for the colonial policies of the Dutch liberals two generations later. By his virtually single-handed establishment of Singapore at the tip of the Malay Peninsula in 1819, Raffles gave to Southeast Asia a new Malacca such as Batavia had never become and to his own country a new sphere of influence in the Malay Peninsula, which speedily became a vital link in the building of a globe-girdling empire.

During the period of the 1820's, the British East India Company fought its first war with Burma and began that process of annexation which by 1885 and through the third Burmese war incorporated Burma into the Indian empire. At the same time the Dutch government, as the reluctant heir of the old Company, floundered, bewildered, under the crushing burden of unwanted empire. Not only was the spirit of the age opposed, but between 1825 and 1830 the Netherlands was forced to fight one of Southeast Asia's longest and most destructive colonial wars against Diponegoro, Prince of the central Javanese state of Djogja-karta. In modern Indonesian nationalist hagiography, Diponegoro is enshrined as a progenitor of the modern independence struggle. Actually, as has happened in many other cases, the Diponegoro revolt was an effort to turn back the clock of history rather than to accelerate its development. In his own personality, Diponegoro personified the complex cultural amalgamation that had taken place on Java. Feeling personal injury because the princely throne had been awarded to a younger brother, he also was motivated by a sense of divinely-inspired mission to restore the ancient glories of Java and drive out the infidel. Although the most puritanical of Islamic believers, he pre-

* Harrison, Brian, *A Short History of South-East Asia.* New York, 1958, p. 173.

pared for his holy war by a process of meditation and self-isolation much as had the Buddha. For the peasants he embodied the ancient legend of the prince-liberator at whose feet the gods had dropped a magic sword from heaven. For elements of the old nobility he represented a rallying point against steady European encroachment.

Before the Java war was ended in 1830, one of Southeast Asia's richest agricultural areas was devastated and some 200,000 lives lost. So dark was the prospect that many responsible Dutch leaders had advocated abandonment of Java as the only solution. The reason that Java instead became the world's prime example of fabulous profits from colonialism was due to one man. What the effect on the future of Southeast Asia might have been if King William had not appointed Gen. van den Bosch as Governor of Java in 1828 offers possibilities for interesting speculation. For van den Bosch by his introduction of the "Culture System" (*cultuur stelsel*) on Java opened the eyes of his European contemporaries to the possibilities inherent in a new type of colonialism, far less risky than the old eighteenth century commercial ventures. It was designed to foster the developing drive of nineteenth century industrial capitalism to integrate the whole earth into one rationalized economic system. Van den Bosch's Culture System provided the pilot project for the rest of Southeast Asia's economic and political development during the remainder of the century.

The essence of the Culture System was simply a far more efficiently organized and supervised application of the methods already used by the Company. The peasant population was required either to devote one-fifth of its arable land to the growing of designated export crops or to contribute sixty-six working days a year by each family head. The Company had been content to set its arbitrary quotas and to leave the methods of fulfillment to the not particularly tender procurement methods of the native aristocracy and of the Chinese, who could lease but not own estates. The same elements were present during the most flourishing period of the Culture System between 1831 and

1877. But Government as opposed to Company control was far more stringently exercised, the "Controller" exercising general supervision not only over economic matters but over native affairs in general. Long before the Ethical Policy of the twentieth century and the much-vaunted, if almost obsessive, paternalism of Dutch colonial administration had set the mold for that curious twentieth century symbiotic love/hate relationship between Dutch and Indonesians, Java was experiencing indirect rule to the maximum. The native regents continued to play a leading role, bound to the status quo by the persuasive ties of sustained power and of economic reward. And there was full opportunity for the Chinese to utilize their managerial and commercial skills.

Over a forty-year period, the Netherlands received the impressive cash return from Java of over eight hundred million guilders (pre-World War II exchange—40 cents U.S.). The Dutch homeland flourished, and its merchant marine became the world's third largest. The same could hardly be said for the colonies. The production of such already profitable export crops as coffee, sugar, and indigo was intensified. In due course, other profitable crops such as tea, tobacco, and cotton were added. For obvious economic reasons, the road system of Java was improved. On the other hand, for the bulk of the native population, those unfortunate social and psychological effects mentioned earlier were intensified. Not surprisingly, each succeeding group of administrators felt compelled to turn the screws a little harder and to pare the governmental expenses for Java a little more to increase the "Indian surplus" (*batig slot*) in the home budget. In view of the sweeping denunciations to which a succeeding generation of liberal humanitarians would subject the Culture System, it is almost as difficult to evaluate it objectively as to form an accurate picture of Catiline's character from the orations of Cicero. It would seem that already by the 1840's the system was inflicting hardship, at times actual starvation, on large masses of the native population. This was due to the increased demands for forced labor and to a

steady encroachment on rice lands—already inadequate
to feed the burgeoning population—for more export crop
area. Whatever the facts, the long-range significance of the
Culture System was its unintentional contribution to economic and social myth-making.

With the demise of the Company in 1799, it had seemed
that the old days of riches in the East were gone. Van den
Bosch demonstrated not only for his own countrymen, but
for other foreign observers as well, that this was not so. In
an era when even Benjamin Disraeli, whose subsequent
career would be linked with the construction of the British
empire, could term colonies in 1851 "these millstones
around our neck," the Dutch financial triumph on Java still
could not be argued away. Nor was the lesson lost on those
enterprising capitalists of the rising European middle class
who by mid-century would be ready to clamor for the
turn of private enterprise to try its luck. On Java by 1870,
the pressures of those conflicting products of liberal philosophy—humanitarianism and private enterprise—had
forced the beginning of the transition from the Culture
System to a new period of liberal laissez-faire. By the beginning of the twentieth century, it would be partly super-
seded by a new paternalistic concept framed in terms of
the so-called "ethical policy."

While the Dutch, in the title words of an account written
by an admiring British observer, were demonstrating "how
to manage a colony," * political and above all economic
pressures were intensifying the process of European empire building throughout all Asia. As the era of commercial
capitalism yielded first in Great Britain, then in the countries of Western Europe, to industrial capitalism with its
need for sources of raw materials and markets for finished
products, the old concepts of purely commercial contacts
were merged almost imperceptibly with the necessity of
political control. And as sails gave way to steam, the
means to do so became increasingly simplified. This was
even more true after the opening of Suez in 1869 with the

* Money, J. W. B., *Java, or How to Manage a Colony*. London, 1861.

shrinkage in communication lines between Western Europe and formerly remote areas.

3. The "Indian Summer" of Colonialism, 1869-1941

Aside from economic and technological pressures, other intangible but highly potent forces were creating a new phase in the relations between Asia and the West which altered both the political map and the destinies of the Southeast Asian peoples far more in the years between 1860 and 1900 than in all the preceding centuries since the first appearance of the Europeans. For these brief decades in the late nineteenth century were the time when, dazzled by the results of their industrial revolution and by the economic and technological superiority it had given them, the western peoples blandly and naively assumed, in the words of H. G. Wells, that it was "a natural and inevitable thing that all the world should fall under European dominion." With varying degrees of actual or assumed reluctance or enthusiasm they prepared to shoulder "the White Man's burden." Not until Japan began to play its curiously ironic role in Asian history were there any developments in European-Asian relations to gainsay this.* Indeed, the total subjection of India, the almost contemptuous humiliation of imperial China, to mention only the two most notable examples, all seemed to demonstrate the inevitability of European domination, however much any particular victim might struggle.

Another intangible but highly important influence in that Europeanization of the world in the second half of the nineteenth century was the grip of nationalism, perhaps the most important of the new forces let loose by the French Revolution. The nineteenth century saw in Western Europe the hysterical apotheosis (again Wells) "of these new and bigger tribal gods—for such indeed, the modern 'nations' are—. . ." In terms of the "glory of the flag" and the "honor of the nation" the European powers utilized their as yet unchallengable technological superiority to divide the

* See p. 62.

world as they saw fit. To the struggle for secure sources of raw materials, for guaranteed markets, for strategic coaling stations, for the fulfillment of the overall European destiny to rule the world was added the almost religious motive of service to the cause of a particular nationalism. Among either tangible or intangible, advertent or inadvertent stimuli to change in Asia made by the Europeans, few if any have been more potent than nationalism. In the nineteenth century, it was the obedient slave of the manifest destiny of the western peoples. In the twentieth it has become a monster which draws increased strength as new nation after nation proudly unfurls its flag. Nationalism has not only shattered the old western colonial system but threatens to do the same to the world itself.

In Southeast Asia, as elsewhere in what we now term "the developing areas," all these forces converged to bring about sweeping changes in the latter half of the nineteenth century. In the mid-1850's, Burma found itself reduced to a landlocked power by the second Anglo-Burman war. And as a result of the third, in 1885 it was annexed to the British Indian empire. Unlike the last two monarchs of independent Burma, the well-intentioned but ineffective Mindon and the weakly degenerate Thibaw, Thailand was fortunate in having three successive monarchs (Rama IV, V, and VI) between 1851 and 1925 whose skill and ability saved their country from western engulfment and created a modern state structure. Where Burma had ignored or scorned relations with the western powers, Thailand sought them and, under its able dynasty, utilized the rivalries of the great powers for its own preservation as a nation. Although it was necessary to cede territory to Britain and, more notably, to the newly created French empire on its eastern borders, Thailand succeeded in maintaining itself largely intact throughout the period of western colonial domination in Southeast Asia.

Using the always convenient gambit of persecuted missionaries in the late 1850's, the new French empire of Napoleon III pushed into Vietnam intent on a cheaply-purchased renewal of imperial glory. In successive bites, beginning with the three eastern provinces of Cochin China (southern Vietnam) in 1862, the French Second Empire and Third Republic by 1884 had effectively established a protectorate over all of Vietnam. As of 1867, France had forced Thailand to relinquish any suzerainty claims over Cambodia, which entered the French sphere. In vain Vietnam or Annam, as it came to be called during the French period, appealed for assistance to China, its nominal political overlord and longtime cultural mentor. In a brief war (1884-1885) China was again humiliated by a western power and forced to recognize the French protectorate over Tonkin, the northernmost province of Vietnam. In 1893, the Indo-Chinese Union, as France had dubbed its new imperial possessions, was rounded off by the declaration of a protectorate over the little mountain kingdoms of Laos. This area had long been in dispute between Vietnam and Thailand, which once again was forced to concede. In terms of the European period in Southeast Asia, this was virtually the first and the last time that the name of Laos would figure prominently in any international developments until the seventh decade of the twentieth century.

Although it had been brought about solely by the accidental developments of great power politics, there was a singular appropriateness in the fact that for the next seventy years the destinies of France and Vietnam were to be closely joined. Each was uniquely culturally prepared to appreciate and to comprehend the other. The French, as did no other European people, valued intellectual achievement and found esthetic reward in the precise use of language, whether written or spoken. And their world of the mind was not enshrouded in the cloudy romance of the Germanic imagination. For the descendants of Descartes and Pascal, it was a place of order, discipline, and rationality with few if any emotional, let alone religious, overtones. It was important not only to think and to have ideas but to be capable of expressing them with style and precision, without undue emotion or passion, and always in terms of *le mot juste*. In the Vietnamese the most sophisticated, traditional, and rational of European peoples met their closest Asian equivalent except for the Chinese.

The Vietnamese represented, above all others, the people and the area of Southeast Asia where the cultural influence of China had been dominant for a period virtually contemporaneous with the Christian era. When in the tenth century of our era the Vietnamese won national independence from China, it had no effect on the Sinic form of their state or, in particular, on their bureaucracy. In Vietnam, as in China itself, intellectual achievement was the key to success and to high government position. There too the mandarinate was the skeleton on which the administrative structure was formed. Implicit in the Vietnamese tradition was the acceptance of the suzerainty of superior power; power not merely superior in military terms but worthy of intellectual respect and emulation as well. In French Indo-China, the intellectualism of the heirs of the Chinese *literati* met and found compatible association with the sceptical rationalism of the heirs of the age of enlightenment.

While it is true, as various commentators have pointed out, that the succeeding French policies of assimilation and association were calculated to have an influence both deeper and broader than the policies pursued by the British and the Dutch, this would seem to be only half the story. It is doubtful that French policy would have succeeded so well with any other Southeast Asian peoples not so culturally and intellectually attuned to accept it as were the Vietnamese. A combination of French racial tolerance and the intellectual compatability of the peoples concerned would seem to explain why it was possible for various Vietnamese during the colonial period, as with no other peoples, to achieve social acceptance and career success within the metropolitan society of the colonizing power itself.

The assimilation concept of creating a small France in Asia was as unrealistic in its way as the association concept, with its failure to provide a meaningful economic basis for an enduring union. Yet, whatever its long-range failure, French policy did create within a much shorter time than in any other colonial area until the American period in the Philippines, a western-acculturated group, notable both in terms of its size, compared to the British and the Dutch equivalents, and in the thoroughness of the results. Yet, for the present ruling elite of Vietnam, it seems to have produced problems from which their Philippine counterparts are largely exempt. In the Philippines the extent of the acculturation was broad enough so that no barrier seems to have been erected between elite and mass: in French Indo-China, the overwhelming mass of the population was quite untouched by the concepts either of assimilation or of association. The apparent result in post-independence Vietnam has been to create in its western-oriented elite an almost compulsive feeling of the necessity to stress the traditional features of the indigenous cultural inheritance as a means of bridging the gap of cultural alienation between themselves and the masses.

By the end of the nineteenth century, the colonial pattern of Southeast Asia had been completed. The Dutch, with grudging reluctance, had finally established effective control over the whole of the Indonesian archipelago, although still utilizing the relatively inexpensive method of indirect rule wherever possible. On this basis, through the shadowy suzerainty claimed over it by the long-time vassal sultanate of Tidore, the western half of the vast island of New Guinea, by agreement with Great Britain and Germany, in 1885, had been included within the boundaries of the Dutch East Indies. In terms of the often-repeated statement about "350 years of Dutch rule in Indonesia," it is worth noting that it was 1908 before Dutch control was fully effective even over the small island of Bali, immediately off Java, and that as late as 1936 it was just being established in sections of the north coast of New Guinea. By the same process all of Borneo except for the sultanates of Brunei and Sarawak plus British North Borneo were added to the Dutch domains.

In Malaya by the turn of the century, the writ of the Queen-Empress ran supreme. This had come about through a typically British process of piecemeal acquisition of territories in an atmosphere of alternating bored indifference, sudden frantic improvisations, and a characteristic pragmatic ability to take the contradictory, the impossible, and the makeshift and then come up, in defiance of all laws of political or administrative gravity, with a finished product which, it could be logically demonstrated, should not work at all yet somehow proceeded to work very well.

Following the founding of Raffles' Singapore in 1819, the British East India Company displayed a notable lack of enthusiasm for extending its writ beyond the new Straits Settlement and its already existing outposts on the west coast, Malacca of historic fame and Penang, Francis Light's 1786 acquisition. Nor, following the liquidation of the Company after the "Indian mutiny" of 1857, did the British government show any particular interest in Malayan expansion. This, however, under the customary pressure of urgent necessity, took place in the 1870's and the 1880's. During this period, the Malay sultanates became protectorates with Great Britain assuming responsibility for law and order. The need for this had not been caused primarily by the Malays themselves, although the traditional practice of piracy continued sporadically until almost the turn of the century. The need for intervention had arisen from the increasing anarchy brought about by the miniature, but bloody, wars fought between rival groups of Chinese tin miners. As early as the 1850's, Chinese merchants in Singapore had been particularly active in exploiting the long-established Malayan tin industry. Since the indigenous Malay population was both inadequate and indifferent to such activities, large numbers of immigrant laborers, particularly from South China, had been imported. By the end of the century, there was a substantial Chinese minority in the Malay states. And in Singapore itself the security offered by British rule had brought about such a concentration of Chinese immigrants that, as early as 1850, they constituted 53 per cent of the population.

The last decades of the nineteenth century saw the growth of those Indian and Chinese minorities in Southeast

Asia which were to offer such a vexing problem for the new nations in the 1950's. Although they are a sizable minority in Malaya (approximately 11 per cent) and in Singapore (over 8 per cent), the Indians have constituted no real minority problem here or elsewhere in Southeast Asia, except in Burma. In Burma, the otherwise ubiquitous Chinese, apparently through colonial control policies, geographical distance, and Indian competition, were never able to gain a foothold. (In 1951, for example, it was estimated that the Chinese minority in Burma constituted only about 1 per cent of the population.)

Even before the final annexation of Upper Burma in 1885, the British Indian government had encouraged Indian immigration to provide both an adequate private and a substantial governmental working force. But it was particularly as a commercial "middle class" that the Indian minority in Burma (only 7 per cent at its peak as of the census of 1931), in the period of the late nineteenth century, had begun to lay the foundations of the solid economic power which was to make them as hated as the Chinese elsewhere. As shopkeepers and, above all, as moneylenders who found it simple to get first the peasant farmer and then his land under their control, the Indian minority prospered during the British period.

Elsewhere in Southeast Asia, where the rise of modern business enterprise, made possible by improved communications and increasingly closer economic ties with world markets, benefited the ruling European minorities, the Chinese were always alert to exploit any opportunities offered them and, for that matter, quite ready and able to create the opportunities for themselves. The social results of Southeast Asia's integration into a world economy were far-reaching. The western impact on the traditional social and economic structure of the area for long had been light. But from approximately 1870, as private capitalist enterprise gathered strength, it greatly increased and smashed the old order beyond repair. In social terms, the customary ties' of family and village were weakened and the magnetic attraction of the new metropolitan centers, created by the administrative and commercial needs of the colonial powers, drew increasing population from the numerous and increasingly debt-ridden peasant masses, the primary victims of the inexorable shift from subsistence to exchange economy. As in British India, the new urban centers of Southeast Asia were to be the incubators for a newly developing, semi-westernized, semi-educated group which had lost contact with the old values and were either unable or frequently were prevented from finding a place for themselves in the new world which was emerging. It was from this embittered and frustrated urban intellectual proletariat that the first nuclei, if not always the leadership, of the nationalist movements would come. As educational opportunities improved, their numbers grew although their sense of angry frustration continued to fester, except in the Philippines.

It continued to be the unique destiny of the Philippines to constitute an exception to developments elsewhere. Until 1898 this had come from the dream-like isolation of Spanish rule. After their transfer to the United States following the Spanish-American war, the reasons were quite otherwise; for the United States entered on its period of empire in Southeast Asia in a fashion unlike any other western power. In the first place, it became a colonial power at the very peak of the period of western domination. There had been no long and gradual development or opportunity for unhurried acclimatization to the idea of empire. Nor did it strain at the possibilities of empire, as did that other latecomer, imperial Germany of the kaisers. From the first, the American attitude towards the Philippines was tinged with a strong feeling of guilt and an intense need for self-justification by the performance of good works. The full missionary zeal of an idealistic people who believed fervently that they held the key to the world's ills was turned on the Philippines. The result, again, was to direct Philippine development into unique channels.

As early as 1899, when the Philippine rebellion against American rule still had three years to run, a mestizo was appointed as the first Chief Justice of the newly-created

Supreme Court; by 1912, half of all ranking judges were Filipino. As of 1907, the lower house of the Philippine Assembly became the first elected legislative body in all of Southeast Asia; and, by 1913, the upper house had acquired a Philippine majority, although it should be noted that substantial control powers, including that of a veto which was hardly ever used, remained in the American governor-general's hands.

In addition to this unique drafting of the native population into participation in self-government, there was the fact that from the beginning American policy envisaged the eventual independence of the Philippines as a desirable result. In a little over one generation (between 1903 and 1939), literacy was doubled and the Filipinos, like the Burmese and the Malayans, enjoyed the fortunate privilege of having English as their second language and thus of possessing a linguistic key to the knowledge of the most influential section of western civilization. In no other colonial area was the knowledge of an important western language more widespread. Just prior to the Japanese war it was estimated that nearly 27 per cent of the entire population was English-speaking. Through the intensive American fostering of a comprehensive educational system, an avenue of social mobility was opened through education. On the debit side of the ledger, however, the American period led to no improvement in the oligarchic concentration of land ownership. Indeed, between 1900 and 1935, the percentage of farm tenants doubled. And the minor peasant revolts, during the twenties and thirties in Central Luzon, provided the handwriting on the wall to warn of this major problem that would plague an independent Philippines.

Although very early in the American period a model civil service law was enacted, the Filipinization of the civil service was pushed so rapidly that the best traditions of the American career administrative service had little chance to be inculcated. Far more dominant were both the indigenous concept of office as an area for family exploitation and the easy-going corruption of the Spanish tradition.

But there was one important, characteristically American, cultural attitude towards government with which the Filipinos became thoroughly imbued and, as a result, acquired a perspective different from that of other Southeast Asian peoples. The governmental priorities of the American period offer a significant key to the difference in cultural attitudes between the United States and the other colonial powers. For the British, French, or Dutch, the primary emphasis was placed on the establishment of a rationalized, western-type administrative structure, operated by a highly-trained and carefully selected corps of career civil servants; only slowly, almost grudgingly, would "natives" be permitted to enter even the outer fringes of this elite group.

For the British and French colonial areas in particular, it did have the effect of creating a very clear-cut authority image—that of the dedicated, non-political, highly-skilled administrator whose "fatherland" was the career civil service. No doubt was left in the minds of any observer as to what were the standards of political conduct or the ultimate goals of the society in question. In Indonesia (the East Indies, to use the colonial designation), this image was considerably blurred by the Dutch system of indirect rule. While ultimate control was no less firmly in the hands of the colonial power, the system of "like over like," continued from the Company period, left unfocused the images of both model political conduct and the ultimate goals. While in British Burma under direct rule, the opposite extreme was represented, Malaya, along with its complex plural society, also represented an equally complicated administrative mixture.

From the beginning, the Straits Settlement of Singapore had represented a venture in direct administration. After the assumption of British control over the peninsular sultanates, four of these were joined in 1895 into a nominal union of the so-called Federated Malay States which were under rather more direct British rule than the other five unfederated sultanates but much less than the Straits Settlement. In Malaya there was virtually every degree of administrative control represented. And there, in microcosm, the impact of western administration varied in direct relation to the intensity and directness of the control exercised, just as in the macrocosmic examples of Burma, Indonesia, and Indo-China.

This idealization of rationalized bureaucracy, particularly in terms of its role as one of the major props of the colonial systems, tended to make it an object of suspicion if not of hostility on the part of the developing western-educated intellectual class. Largely barred from responsible roles and frequently operating under a heavy-handed security surveillance, political activity for them became a matter of intense ideological allegiances, with the forbidden but compellingly magic goal of independence as their leading article of faith. The politician's role was seen not as that of the mediator and reconciler of conflicting interests, but rather in terms of an absolutist ideological crusader perpetually in opposition and, hence, removed from the necessity of facing the sobering responsibilities of power and decision-making.

In the Philippines after 1898, the very essence of the American concept of government as deriving its stimuli and policy directives from the decisions of elected representatives led to the creation of a very different authority myth from that which, in varying degree, served as model elsewhere in Southeast Asia. Not the career administrator, but the elected representative, the career politician, was held up to the Philippine people as the vital connecting link in the relationship between the voters and "their" government. Furthermore, again in the American image, the career politician was conceived of as a profoundly un-ideological adjuster of conflicting interests within the society.

There was, indeed, little on which to base any ideological crusade; the achievement of ultimate independence was axiomatic. The only issue involved was one of timing. And far from being excluded from office and responsibility, the Filipino politician frequently found himself being shoved into it before he was entirely ready. His role was to find a harmonious basis on which, after skillful haggling and shrewd bargaining, the interests of his particular group of clients could be reconciled with others. From the first, the

Philippine politician has had no reason to feel any sense of alienation. Nor have the political parties, encouraged to organize themselves even before American rule was consolidated, ever possessed that ideological character found elsewhere in Southeast Asia. As in the United States, their programs have been strongly pragmatic with differences centering not on conflicting world views but rather on questions of timing and emphasis. One has only to compare the political history since independence of Indonesia and the Philippines to grasp the significant difference made by the "style" of the colonial administration involved in the political outlooks and concepts of peoples of essentially similar racial background.

By the first decade of the twentieth century, the western colonial system in Southeast Asia seemed established on a Gibraltar-like foundation destined to endure for generations to come. Except for Thailand, every area of Southeast Asia was neatly colored in red or blue or yellow to indicate that it was part of some world-wide empire. Economically, the region was thoroughly integrated into world economy. As the twentieth century added years, even more than in the days of the sixteenth century, the "treasure house of the Indies" became reality. Blessed by nature with one of the world's most fecund soils and equable climates, highly organized under the plural economy system of western enterprise with production for world markets superimposed on the old peasant subsistence economy, and possessed of an abundance of cheap manpower, Southeast Asia and especially Indonesia poured forth a rich stream of agricultural products. Increasingly it was discovered that the area was rich in mineral resources. The tin mines of Malaya had been known since time immemorial, but the needs of twentieth century technology led to the discovery of other equally important resources. The combination of agricultural and mineral resources of Southeast Asia made a long and impressive list.

From Indonesia alone, in order of importance, in the period just before the Second World War, were exported rubber, petroleum, vegetable oils, tin, sugar, tea, quinine, spices, kapok, coffee, and other agricultural products. For its small size, Malaya proved itself a uniquely profitable treasure house with its flourishing rubber and tin enterprises plus the commercial magnet of Singapore. Burma became the world's leading producer of tungsten and led all of Asia in exports of silver and lead. In addition to a small but highly profitable oil industry, Burma's forests yielded teakwood as an important export item. In addition, Burma along with Thailand and French Indo-China each year produced a large export rice crop, which found ready markets in rice-deficient Indonesia and Malaya. From 1914 on, the Philippines, shaking off the centuries of the Spanish trance under the stimulus of increasing American investments, became an important and protected supplier of hemp, tobacco, sugar, and copra to the American market.

Perhaps the most striking characteristic common to the economies of all the "new" nations was the lack of any extensive industrial development. In part this was attributable to the economic policies followed by the former colonial powers. Throughout the period of European domination, from the time of the initial Dutch-Portuguese struggle for control of the Moluccan spice trade to the time of the Japanese conquest, Southeast Asia had been viewed as a valuable source of raw materials. In the nineteenth century, as Europe's economic life moved from the commercial into the industrial phase, Southeast Asia became important not only as a treasure house of raw materials but as a market area for the sale of finished products. In all fairness to the colonial powers, however, it should be pointed out that, aside from the factor of not deliberately creating competition for their home industries, there was much sound economic justification for continuing Southeast Asia's traditional role as a supplier of raw materials. The iron and coal necessary for modern industrialism is largely lacking. And quite aside from the problem of technological training, there is no industrially-oriented labor force.*

In Java, Malaya, and the Philippines, for example,

* The training programs of American oil companies seem to have rendered valuable service during recent years.

processing industries have long been present, but these too have been simply links in the preparation of the raw product for shipment abroad. Southeast Asia has not only been linked with world economy but, increasingly in the era of industrial capitalism, it has been placed at the mercy of the fluctuations of its economic cycles. As vexatious as this situation is for the new nations, both in economic and psychological terms, the great mass of the peasant populations remain unaffected. Rice and fish continue as the staple diet and subsistence agriculture and fishing as the major occupations for the masses. In terms of its influence on economic development, it would seem that a far more important factor than the lack of opportunities offered by European entrepreneurs has been the disinterest, if not complete unawareness, of the overwhelming mass of the population, both now and in the past, in the implications of a monetary economy. The tiny native entrepreneurial class that began to develop just before the Second World War found itself handicapped both by lack of capital and by the highly professional competition of the Chinese and the Indian merchants who were on a low enough level to constitute an initial block to native entrepreneurial efforts.

But, as with the peasant masses, there was little interest in commerce or business enterprise on the part of the aristocracy. Its interests and values were oriented in intellectual bureaucratic terms. In Java and Indo-China the old bureaucratic elite found continued employment for their talents under the European regimes. But even as a more westernized native intellectual group developed, its values were not materially different. Its members, initially at least, the sons, and sometimes the daughters, of the old aristocracy were well-grounded in the philosophy, the history, the literature, and especially the political thinking of the West. But for most, its technological and particularly commercial and financial techniques were subjects which aroused little interest either in terms of study or of career. In part, this was certainly due to the limited possibilities offered by the colonial systems, but a powerful negative cultural tradition was also an important factor.

As occurred in India perhaps thirty years earlier, western education became increasingly a status symbol for the newly emerging elite, and, in most cases, the determining factor in recruitment of the developing nationalist movements. Almost alone among the Southeast Asian peoples, the Filipinos showed an ability to adjust to the new commercial and industrial possibilities. In part this may have been due to the solid economic foundaions and managerial experience acquired by the long-established, land-owning families. But also present was the unique factor of an open and largely unrestricted political atmosphere in which the concept of eventual independence was no Holy Grail to be pursued by perilous quest but a routine certainty. In Malaya and Burma, the new elite studied law; and in Indonesia, with the Dutch emphasis on engineering and medicine,* these constituted the ranking status indication of westernized education. Probably under French schooling and as a deliberate policy, young Vietnamese intellectuals received a broader and more thorough grounding in western culture and civilization than did any other group.

Again with the exception of the Philippines, basic career objectives were almost obsessively focused on bureaucratic or on intellectual careers of some sort. At best the possibilities were limited. This was particularly true in Indonesia, where the government followed a deliberate policy of reserving lower-level governmental and clerical posts for the large Eurasian minority. But nowhere did opportunities exist in sufficient volume to satisfy even a small number of those who sought them. And even for those who were successful, bitterness and disillusionment were still fre-

* As early as 1851 the Dutch had established the first school (the STOVIA of Bandung) in East Asia offering medical education on a western basis while in 1913 and 1928 respectively "the Dutch East Indies Doctor's School" and a dental school were established. In 1920 the Technological University of Bandung was founded some four years before the establishment of the College of Law. Anyone familiar with the Indonesian nationalist movement is aware of the high percentage of its leaders who bore either medical or engineering ("Ir."—*ingenieur*) titles.

quently in store. For western education did not prove to be an automatic key to a greatly enhanced economic and social status. The most obvious scapegoats were the colonial regimes. For the alienated, underemployed, and embittered new intellectual class, its untried and naïve values fed by an intoxicating brew of Jeffersonianism and Marxism, the answer seemed simple: it was only necessary to bring the colonial regimes down and automatically all wrongs would be righted.

But it is indicative of the mold in which Southeast Asia had been cast by the colonial period that almost never, until virtually the very end, was there any effort toward or awareness of the desirability of cooperation between the various colonial nationalist movements. Economically, politically, and culturally Southeast Asia had become thoroughly compartmentalized. The young Burmese intellectual used English as his second language and the London School of Economics was his cultural influence. His Vietnamese counterpart argued modern art in the sidewalk cafés of Paris in fluent French, while the young Javanese aristocrat struggled through the severity of both Delft's engineering school and the Dutch winter climate. Each of these would have felt uncomfortable in the chief city of any of the others; and all, as postwar developments have shown, would feel ill-at-ease with the Filipinos. The Hague-Batavia, Paris-Saigon, London-Rangoon axes of colonial Southeast Asia in economic, cultural, and political terms have shown themselves since 1945 to be made of tough material, surprisingly impervious even to such violent stresses and strains as Dutch-Indonesian relations have experienced over the past twenty years.

As seemingly overwhelmingly powerful as the colonial structure appeared at the turn of the twentieth century, only a brief five years passed before there was a significant indication, for those who stopped to note it, that a new era in relations between the western and non-western peoples had begun. For western observers, the broader implications of the event in question were largely unrealized. For the peoples of Asia, the reaction to Japan's crushing military victory over Tzarist Russia, as duly certified in the American-sponsored treaty of Portsmouth in September, 1905, was quite otherwise. A historian of India quotes a contemporary Turkish observed as commenting, "A stir of excitement passed over the North of India. Even the remote villages talked over the victories of Japan as they sat in their circles and passed around the *huqqa* at night . . . Asia was moved from one end to the other, and the sleep of centuries was finally broken." *

Although this account applies to India, it would seem equally appropriate for Southeast Asia. For it was precisely in the years following the Japanese shattering of the myth of western invincibility that the nationalist movements of Southeast Asia began to appear. Cause and effect in such matters are difficult to prove, and no doubt there were many contributory factors, above all the increasing emergence of the new western-educated elite of which we have spoken earlier. But it is significant that it was after the Japanese victory that the Southeast Asian nationalist movements, again with the Philippines as the exception, appeared on the scene. In the Philippines it will be recalled, with its essentially Latin American rather than Southeast Asian pattern, the nationalist movement had asserted itself at such an early date that by the mid-1890's it could muster sufficient strength to launch open rebellion against Spanish rule.

Elsewhere in Southeast Asia the first faint and modest beginnings of the modern nationalist movements occurred in Burma and Java, the traditional center for activity of any sort in the Indonesian archipelago. In both cases the initial nationalist stirrings were non-political in nature and dedicated to a revival of traditional values. In Burma, the Buddhist Young Men's Association, founded in 1906, sought to reinterpret the basic values of Buddhism in terms of the modern western impact. In Java a small group of aristocrats held the first meeting in 1908 of the *Budi Utomo* (High Endeavor) society, dedicated to essentially the same

* Wallbank, T. Walter, *A Short History of India and Pakistan.* New York, 1958, p. 107.

goals. But as early as 1912, Indonesia in the Sarekat Islam (the Islamic Association) had produced the region's first mass political movement, motivated by resentment of both the European and especially the Chinese monopolies over economic and commercial life. Although in Indo-China the psychological impact of the Russo-Japanese War produced an abortive and mismanaged revolutionary conspiracy as early as 1906 (the so-called Gilbert Chieu conspiracy), it was not until the post-World War I period that a nationalist movement as such began to develop in Vietnam or, for that matter, in Burma.

Although in Malaya during the twenties and thirties there was conflict within the Malayan population between the modernists and the traditionalists, the racial pluralism of the colony plus the wide spectrum of political power prevented the emergence of a nationalist movement as such until the Japanese World War II occupation. For the Malayan Chinese during this period, the only events of interest were those taking place in the homeland where, from the beginning of the decade of the thirties, China was engaged in the desperate struggle for survival against Japanese aggression.

In Thailand, Southeast Asia's one independent state until after World War II, the stimulus of the Japanese victory of 1905 seems to have had an important effect in the creation of a modern concept of nationalism, which found expression in Thai resentment against European economic and political domination and against the ubiquitous Chinese commercial influence. As in both Burma and Indonesia, traditional religious values were equated with the new nationalism at the same time that strenuous efforts were made, particularly in the 1930's, to westernize many aspects of social and cultural activities. A particularly interesting aspect of the development of the Thai nationalist movement was the bloodless shift in political power brought about in 1932. In June of that year the new western-educated Thai middle class seized power from the monarchy and the princely clique surrounding it. Prominent in the new group was a brilliant young Parisian-trained lawyer, Pridi Banomyong, whose name was to appear and reappear in the political history of his nation from that date thence. Significantly, the coup was made possible by the support received from a group of western-trained middle-level army officers. It was a precedent which, in the Southeast Asia of the 1950's, would become a familiar pattern. The shift in power which occurred in 1932, although with ironic overtones, provided proof positive of the success with which the Ramas had accomplished their modernizing task.

After, as before, 1932 the monarchy continued to be the visible symbol of the nation. The chief difference was that power, henceforth, rested in the hands of a small civilian-military oligarchy instead of the prolific royal family. From 1932 until now, the political history of Thailand has been largely the tale of the fallings in and fallings out of the members of this group. Continuing the Thai tradition of skillful diplomatic maneuvering, its members brought Thailand into the Second World War on the side of Japan in time to prevent either hostile invasion or damage.* At war's end, through the accession to power of a leading member of the anti-Japanese Free Thai underground movement, Thailand, as had Italy in Europe, succeeded in tempering the winds of change and ending up substantially with the territory it had possessed at the war's beginning. Since 1945, Thailand has drawn increasingly closer to the United States, the nation chiefly responsible for its lenient treatment in the peace treaties. Although Thailand joined the Southeast Asia Treaty Organization (SEATO) in 1954 as one of the only two (the other being the Philippines) Southeast Asian states to do so, there were increasing signs in the early sixties that, as American and western prestige continued to sink in Southeast Asia, the highly perceptive Thai political radar was picking up signals from the communist bloc. Coupled with a well-justified traditional fear of China as an imperialist power is Thailand's concern with its large (approximately 2,300,000 in a total population of

* Technically the Japanese did invade Thailand but not as enemies.

22,800,000) and economically dominant Chinese minority.

Beyond our scope is any detailed examination of developments in the colonial areas of Southeast Asia in the years of the twentieth century before 1941. It is a curious irony of history that twice in a little more than a generation it has been Japan's unrewarding destiny to be the catalyst for change in Asia. In 1905, it was Japan which broke the spell of the predestined invincibility of the West; and again in 1941, it was Japan which shattered the old colonial regimes and thus signalled the close of the Vasco da Gama era in Asian-African and in world history.

After 1901, Dutch administration in Indonesia was conducted in terms of the "Ethical Policy" proclaimed in the Queen's Throne speech of that year. Its basic principle was the concept of benevolent paternalism towards the native population. Although it brought improved economic and welfare conditions (Java's population, for example, increased from 23,000,000 in 1890 to over 40,000,000 in 1930), it kept the Indonesians in the role of passive beneficiaries. Even a Peoples' Council (Volksraad) established in 1918, in contrast to the slow but steady training in governmental participation given in the British areas, remained little more than an ineffective debating society regarded with scorn by the nationalist movement. As early as 1920 the Indonesian Communist Party became Southeast Asia's first official communist group. It was not until 1925 that a brilliant young Moscow-trained Vietnamese, best known under the name of Ho Chi Minh, formed the first cell group of the Association of Revolutionary Annamite Youth among his compatriots living in South China. Elsewhere in the area, communism as an organized force achieved little importance until after World War II.

A badly-timed and foredoomed communist revolt in Java in 1926-27 led to the suppression of all aspects of the nationalist movement for the remainder of the colonial period. In Indo-China, equally ill-timed nationalist and communist revolts led to the same result. Divided by its polyglot population and mixed governmental systems, Malaya remained a tranquil colony until the Japanese conquest. Only in Burma, where in the period between the wars increasing progress was made towards self-government, and in the Philippines, which, under the provisions of the Tydings-McDuffie Act of 1934, became a commonwealth with independence promised ten years later, did any real changes take place in the functioning of the colonial system in Southeast Asia in the period prior to the Japanese occupation of the area.

4. The Japanese Period, 1942-1945

Quite aside from the deathblow it dealt the colonial system in Southeast Asia, the Japanese period (1942-1945) was important for other reasons. Although different areas were administered by the Japanese army or navy or civilians, Southeast Asia, for the first time in its history, was united under one authority. The old exclusive lines of communication between London and Paris and The Hague and their colonial areas were snapped and, under the intensive Japanese propaganda of "Asia for the Asians," a psychological reorientation took place. What only a few years before had seemed the visionary and chimerical dreams of frequently suppressed and often numerically small nationalist movements suddenly had become reality. Solely for their own purposes, the Japanese made use of the nationalist movements. As early as August, 1943, Japan established a technically independent Burma, followed in October by the proclamation of a so-called "Philippine Republic." It was not until almost the very end of the war, the spring months of 1945, that Japan encouraged similar steps in Indonesia. In March, 1945, an Investigating Committee for the Preparation of Independence was established, although an Indonesian auxiliary "army" had been created by the Japanese as early as 1943.

To what extent the various nationalist movements made use of, rather than believed in, the Japanese is still in question. The Indonesian nationalist leaders, for example, when courting American sympathy in the postwar period, were insistent on the official thesis of an elaborate and well-planned preconceived strategy which saw some seemingly cooperating with the "fascist invaders" while others led underground resistance. In varying degrees the same pattern appeared in Burma and in the Philippines. It seems reasonable to conjecture that initially there was much enthusiasm for the Japanese cause and a considerable degree of spontaneous cooperation, even in the Philippines. Again, it seems logical to assume that as the surprising inability of the Japanese to comprehend their fellow Asians, their brutality, and the mounting demands for forced labor became more and more routine under the increasingly obvious shadow of defeat, admiration turned to hate and cooperation to an enmity that saw the Japanese-trained Burmese army fighting with the allies at war's end.

But as ruinous as the Japanese period (1942-1945) in Southeast Asia was for Nippon itself, it was the making of the nationalist movements. Without benefit of such a cataclysmic period of change, it would have taken decades to reach the positions in which they found themselves in 1945. This was particularly true in Indonesia. The banning of the Dutch language gave impetus to the use of the Indonesian. The purging from government service not only of Dutch officials but the unusually large number of Eurasians in subordinate positions opened up greatly improved job opportunities and new training in administrative skills. The nationalist leaders were freed from prison camps. All these factors were of incalculable value to the Indonesian nationalist movement. Indeed, it is not without significance that it was the first former colony in Southeast Asia to proclaim itself an independent nation. On August 17, 1945, two days after the Japanese surrender, under the leadership of Sukarno, who is still president, and Mohammed Hatta, who was vice-president until his split with Sukarno in 1956, an independent Indonesian Republic was proclaimed in Batavia which was promptly renamed Djakarta. The stage was set for a bitter and gruelling four-year independence struggle.

5. *Contemporary Southeast Asia, 1945-*

The complex, sometimes tragic, sometimes sensational, always accelerating series of events which, except for a few scattered enclaves, had liquidated the colonial system in Southeast Asia within a decade of war's end can be surveyed only in broad perspective. Perhaps this perspective can best be gained if, for perhaps the last time, we view it in terms of the colonial powers rather than of the indigenous peoples. A famous British student of American affairs of an earlier generation (Lord Bryce) is credited with the observation that a special providence looks after fools, children, and the United States of America. A survey of British imperial history (or the lack of it) in the years immediately following the Second World War would seem to offer convincing arguments for including the destinies of Lord Bryce's own nation under the aegis of that special providence.

For it seems most unlikely that, had the British Conservatives under the leadership of the great Churchill still been in power during the years between 1945 and 1950, Mr. Churchill would have been any more willing as prime minister to preside over the liquidation of His Majesty's Empire than when he originally uttered his famous disavowal to that effect some years earlier. If not an act of that special providence, it was a matter of happy coincidence that the election results of 1945 brought Labor into power precisely when the problem of the enforced liquidation of empire was the prime agenda item of the day. With its long-standing anti-colonial outlook, the British Labor Party was the ideal governing group to undertake this task. It is again one of those curious British good fortunes that in so doing it was able to make nothing so distinguish British imperial power as the graceful manner of its leaving and thus create a new and unique bond between Britain and its former colonies.

In Burma by 1943, disillusionment with the realities of existence in the Greater East Asia Co-Prosperity Sphere had led to the creation of the Anti-Fascist Peoples' Freedom League (AFPFL) which, like the Indian Congress Party, has dominated the national scene ever since. By negotiation with the British Labor Government the AFPFL, which in the constituent assembly elections of 1947 emerged as the overwhelmingly dominant political force (172 of 182 seats), Burma was brought to the world stage as an independent nation on January 4, 1948, at the astrologically guaranteed hour of 3:40 A.M. (In terms of the persistence of cultural heritage, it is not without interest that the astrologers in question were, in this plus 80 per cent Buddhist nation, Brahmins, the priestly caste of the Hindu faith.) Burma opted to leave the Commonwealth of Nations, but British-Burmese relations, although they have had their periods of tension and strain, have never constituted a major problem for either country. This contrasts, for example, with the obsessive preoccupation with each other's deficiencies and real or fancied betrayals of faith that have been characteristic of the unhappy diplomatic relations that have existed from the beginning between the Netherlands and independent Indonesia.

Even though Burma was no more able to escape the tensions of the mounting Cold War than was any other nation, domestic rather than foreign problems dominated the first decade of its existence as an independent nation. It was a violent and bloody experience which began with mass assassination of government leaders even before independence and then moved on into a protracted phase of multiple revolts and chaos. In July, 1947, just three months after the overwhelming election victory of the AFPFL, its leader, Aung San, and six other leading party figures were assassinated by political opponents. It was Burma's good fortune that, in spite of this crushing loss, an extraordinarily able man, U (a traditional Burmese title of respect) Nu, then vice-president of the AFPFL, was present to succeed him and—except for a two-and-a-half-year period in the late 1950's—to serve continuously thereafter as the nation's leader. Apparently without personal ambition and possessed of high integrity, Nu is a devoutly practicing

Buddhist and, in the social democratic sense, was formerly and simultaneously a dedicated Marxist.*

From the first days of its existence, Burma's new government was forced to fight for life against revolts by two varieties of communist dissidents (Red Flag and White Flag Communists), the Karen and the Shan minorities, with the latter group receiving support from remnants of the defeated Chiang Kai-shek military forces who had fled into Burma.

In spite of this chaotic situation, Burma's first election, held in 1952, continued the hegemony of the AFPFL. As the various revolts were increasingly smothered by the government's military and propaganda actions, the second national election of 1956 again returned the dominant party. But this time the opposing National Unity Front (NUF) scored important gains. In October, 1958, following a split in the AFPFL, widespread charges of governmental corruption, and rising public uncertainty and unrest, U Nu resigned as prime minister, handing his powers of government to the commander of the Burmese army, General Ne Win. Following a pattern already familiar—notably in Egypt and Pakistan—the army group, dominated by young officers, was successful in carrying out a program of extensive reform. This was rather surprisingly climaxed by the Army's voluntary surrender of power to U Nu after his "clean" AFPFL had swept the elections held under Army auspices in February, 1960. On again assuming office as Prime Minister, U Nu praised the army for its house-cleaning reforms and patriotic selflessness and pledged adequate safeguards to prevent his again dominant party (now known as the Union [Pyidaungsu] Party) from being corrupted by the fruits of power.

But Burma's return to the patterns of constitutional democracy proved short-lived indeed. In early March, 1962, General Ne Win again seized power, alleging as justifica-

* The sobering responsibilities of power went far to dim the Marxist enthusiasms of Nu and the other AFPFL leaders. Nu now seems dedicated to Buddhism as the basis for modern Burmese unification.

tion the "greatly deteriorating conditions in the Union" and U Nu's "hesitant attitude towards trade and other problems." Although Parliament was dissolved, the political parties were permitted to function provided that they engage in no hostile activity against the new regime. The establishment of an Army-dominated National Revolutionary Council as the chief governing body for the nation seemed to indicate that this time there was no intent on the part of the military to relinquish power after a short period of national house cleaning. Again a venture in the operation of a western-type democracy had been abandoned by an Asian nation.

In so doing, Burma found itself following what seemed to be the basic pattern of development of the decade of the sixties; for, under different circumstances, much the same course had been followed by Indonesia, potentially the most important among the new nations of Southeast Asia. The difficulties and hardships of Indonesia's struggle for independence were exceeded only by the Vietnamese experience. But unlike Burma, Indonesia, more than a decade after the formal withdrawal of the Dutch, has not been able to find itself as a nation.

The Dutch returned to Indonesia in late 1945 determined to resume, in the title words of an official survey of Dutch colonialism in the twentieth century, their *Mission Interrupted* at precisely the point where the Japanese had forced its (in the Dutch view) temporary suspension. Still firmly convinced that these "childlike people" could not possibly function without their indefinitely continued firm but kind supervision, the Dutch, unlike the British, doggedly dedicated themselves to the resumption of a divinely-inspired national "mission," as an influential and uniquely religiously-oriented section of Dutch opinion saw it.

During a traumatic four-year period of endless negotiations, beautifully drafted legalistic statements of "final settlements"—which were outmoded by events before the wax had hardened on their official seals, and desperate attempts to crush the independence movement by military force, Holland with increasing frustration sought recovery of its colonial empire. By the end of 1949, however, the Indonesian Republic, centered on central Java and often referred to as the Djogja Republic from its capital city, led by Sukarno and Hatta, aided by U.N. and American diplomatic pressure, forced reluctant Dutch acceptance of Indonesian independence.

The price paid by the new United States of Indonesia included the acceptance of membership in a so-called Dutch-Indonesian Union which, in a ponderously (and characteristically) legalistic fashion, represented a desperate Dutch effort to salvage something from the wreckage of empire with the creation of a British type of commonwealth arrangement by administrative fiat, rather than by evolutionary development. The Union, which, again with unimaginative tactlessness, was to be permanently headed by the Dutch sovereign, constituted from the first one of the major reasons for the mutually frustrating and sterile relationship which the two nations have continuously experienced.

Another major barrier to the type of fruitful cooperation which has grown between Great Britain and its former colonies is the "Irian" question. The exigencies of internal politics and a grim determination to retain some fragment of empire caused the Dutch in 1949 when they finally acknowledged Indonesian independence, to continue to rule over the western half of the vast island of New Guinea. This island had been formally acquired, although never effectively occupied, as a result of hegemony over the East Moluccan sultanate of Tidore, which had established a shadowy claim to the area. As the heir to the former Netherlands Indies, Indonesia has never ceased to press its claim to West Irian, the Indonesian name.

The Dutch, still asserting a concept of moral mission, have continued in effective occupation of West New Guinea. The publically stated basis for Dutch retention of West Irian has been that the primitive peoples concerned need continued tutelage and are racially different from the "Indonesians," although the latter already include, as noted earlier, some fifty-four distinct ethnic groups. As the

Burmese representative to the Eleventh General Assembly of the U.N. in 1957 pointed out, the British could have used the same argument to insist on maintaining a protectorate over the Shan, the Kareni, and other backward hill peoples in Burma and thus retained an imperial foothold.

But in spite of both the duration and the bitterness of the Irian dispute, as of 1962 its settlement in the near future seemed a likely probability. Early in the year, Indonesia, after repeated warnings, had resorted to an increasingly accelerated policy of guerilla infiltration and other military measures to bring pressure on the Dutch. By mid-January, acting UN Secretary-General U Thant had persuaded both parties to accept mediation. As of March, at the "suggestion" of the State Department, in a procedure similar to that used to settle the original Indonesian-Dutch dispute, talks had begun between the two nations with American ex-ambassador Bunker present, at the suggestion of U Thant, as a "third party." In spite of various reservations raised by both sides, it seemed as of mid-June, 1962, that Southeast Asia's oldest colonial problem was headed for settlement on the basis of the so-called "Bunker proposals" providing for a transitional interim one- to two-year period of UN trusteeship between Dutch withdrawal and the transfer of West Irian to Indonesia. In essence, with the liquidation of the Irian problem, colonialism seemed likely to become a very minor issue indeed in Southeast Asia. For, of the remaining colonial areas, there seemed little doubt but that the British areas of Borneo would achieve independent status in the near future while Portuguese rule over the half million inhabitants of otherwise Indonesian Timor continues as yet not seriously challenged through its fourth slumberous century.

The obsessive quarrel with Holland, including the Dutch economic domination which the Indonesian nationalists felt still bound them in a subtle but effective framework of colonialism, has never ceased to be an unsettling element in Indonesia's national existence. All too many other problems have continued unsolved for all too many years. One of the most serious of these has been the lack of consensus, from which the Indonesian nationalist movement has suffered from the beginning of the revolutionary period in 1945. Neither in terms of a widely encompassing dominant party such as the Indian Congress or the Burmese AFPFL, nor in terms of the implicit western-type of constitutional consensus involved in the Philippine political system where parties compete in terms of techniques not ideologies, has Indonesia ever been able to resolve this conflict. From 1945 until now it has made difficult, often impossible, the resolution of other important problems; for nations, like men, cannot plot their courses without an accepted way of life. This, as of the 1960's, Indonesia has still to find.

In part, but only in part, the blame could be placed on Dutch twentieth-century colonial policy. Often with dedicated and idealistic intent on the part of the officials concerned, this policy carefully sheltered Indonesia from the frequently brutal impact of the modern world. Yet neither in intent nor in practice had it ever tried to exclude totally all of its native subjects from any degree of contact. If contrast be desired, it is perhaps appropriate to say that where the French overexposed their native elite to westernization, the Dutch underexposed. But this underexposure was not consistent in terms of the whole of the indigenous upper class. Those members of it who were willing to abjure all allegiance to the "native" world and to meet the highly exacting Dutch standards of western culture and knowledge had the possibility, if not the probability, of being able to do so. But for those who chose to remain "traditional" in their world view and sense of values, there was also an equal place. The result was to leave the Indonesians with a blurred and conflicting image of authority as such, and without consensus on governmental organization.

During their period of occupation, the Japanese made adept use of these already existing divisions in the nationalist movement. Not only did they foster a secular movement in conflict with one which desired an independent Indonesia to be an Islamic state, but within the religious movement a split was fostered between the modernists and the traditionalists. During the revolutionary period (1945-1949) yet a third current, based on Marxism, appeared. The Indonesian Communist Party (PKI), following its suppression after the 1926-27 revolt, had not been able to revive until late in the Japanese period. After 1945, under the stimulus of the national revolutionary situation, the party experienced rapid growth only to rush headlong once again, at Madium in 1948, into armed revolt, this time against the Indonesian Republic. The effect of the debacle was to discredit the PKI for some years thereafter, although by the 1955 national election it was the fourth largest party in the nation. It had staged a surprising comeback. This trend continued on Java in subsequent municipal council elections.

The antagonisms between and among the various ideological and political groupings, never too well suppressed even at times of maximum danger during the revolution itself, burst into the open after independence. As the masses lapsed into their traditional passivity, politics, like administration before it, became the occupation of a few thousand upper-class elite. Their personal likes and dislikes and family relationships tended to influence events as much as, if not more than, ideological alliances. In the Philippine sense, there was little wealth in most of their backgrounds; furthermore virtually all of them equated capitalism with colonialism. It was not so much a question of whether any particular party among the eighteen which were represented in the appointed House of Representatives was socialist or nationalist, but rather in what particular way. The variations ranged from the outright, if conflicting, communist positions of the PKI and the nationalist communist Murba (Proletarian) Party through the over-westernized and too-sophisticated social-democratic concepts of the intellectuals of the Indonesian Socialist Party; to the rice-roots proletarian nationalism (*marhaenism*) of the Sukarno-favored Nationalist Party; to the Islamic socialism of the modern-minded major religious party, the Masjumi. In 1952, the traditionalist section in the Islamic community broke off from Masjumi to form the Nahdatul

Ulama (League of Moslem Teachers), which emerged from the 1955 elections with an unexpected 18 per cent of the vote as opposed to the 16 per cent of the Communists and the slightly over 20 per cent each of the Masjumi and the Nationalists. One result of the 1955 elections was to indicate that, except for the Masjumi, the other parties all found their chief support on overpopulated Java (2/3 of the nation's population on 1/15 of the land area).

During the decade of the fifties, Indonesia experienced an uninhibited political Mardi gras. With few exceptions its revolutionary leaders entered upon independence, after the long years of prison, exile, physical danger, and revolutionary travail, with much the same emotions as Charles II, when, after the years of exile and poverty, he mounted the English throne with the superfluous exhortation to his faithful companions, "Let us now enjoy ourselves."

The poly-party division of the representative body ensured that multi-party cabinets would be necessary. The perennial antagonism between the major parties ensured that no cabinet could hope to survive unduly long—there were eight between 1950 and mid-1959, one of which (the strongly Sukarno-supported, Nationalist Party-dominated cabinet of Ali Sastroamidjojo) lasted for almost two years between 1953 and 1955. In the course of the constant cabinet reshuffling various parties staked out fiefs for their faithful in particular ministries, and the bureaucracy swelled from the 145,000 needed by the Dutch in 1930 to administer the affairs of approximately 60,000,000 Indonesians to 600,000 by 1953 for a population of approximately 75,000,000. By 1960, the estimated figures were 1,000,000 with a population of about 90,000,000. The 1955 elections, long heralded as a panacea for Indonesia's political ills, solved nothing. By 1957 the nation existed in terms of permanent political, economic, social, and internal security crises.

In part, the political crises arose from the premature but understandable effort to organize Indonesian political life on the basis of a sophisticated western parliamentary system requiring long evolutionary development and consensus for its successful operation; in part, it arose from the enigmatic role played by Indonesia's great revolutionary leader and permanent president, Sukarno. Possessed of unique charisma and an ability at spellbinding oratory, Sukarno was the ideal leader for the independence struggle. Like many another great revolutionary, all else was anticlimax. As the seductive corruptions of unlimited power, unceasingly flattered vanity, and constantly catered appetites worked their unhappy results, Sukarno increasingly became the indispensable but essentially destructive force in Indonesia's national existence.

Bored by the undemanding symbolic job of president in a parliamentary system, Sukarno's backstage manipulations played no small role in the making and unmaking of cabinets, the rise and fall of political careers. The President came to equate himself with Indonesia and to see opposition to the one as treason to the other. The Nationalists and, as they increasingly sang his praises, the once-distrusted Communists became his favorite parties while the Masjumi and Socialists, under leaders such as Mohammed Natsir and Sutan Sjahrir, who as prime ministers had opposed Sukarno, became objects of suspicion and hostility. By 1957, as Indonesia's crisis worsened, the President became increasingly disenchanted with western democracy.

Economic decline was no small part of the problem. Potentially the richest of Southeast Asia's new nations, by the mid-1950's governmental extravagance and sheer incompetence had reduced Indonesia to a state of chronic bankruptcy endurable only because of the large proportion of its population still living on a sustenance basis. For the city masses, in particular the middle classes, the spiralling inflation brought increasing misery and discontent. Nor was the economic situation helped any by widely scattered and constantly recurring outbreaks of murder, pillage, and plantation destruction by armed bands, sometimes politically motivated, sometimes simply bandits. In West Java, for example, a fanatical Islamic group known as the Darul-Islam (D.I.) has been waging war against the Djakarta government for the establishment of an Islamic state ever since 1949. Elsewhere in the outlying regions of Indonesia there were various other rebellions, sometimes linked with the D.I., sometimes motivated by resentment over the Javanese domination of governmental posts and virtual monopoly as beneficiary of government revenues—mostly furnished by other areas of the nation.

By 1957 the Army became involved in these regional revolts. Earlier in 1952 various elements of the Army had made brief sorties in politics. But in 1957 regional commanders, often from the areas in question, began forming regional councils which refused cooperation with the Sukarno-supported, Nationalist Party-dominated, second Ali cabinet. The disapproving resignation the previous year of Vice-President Hatta, who increasingly had looked askance at Sukarno's leftist nationalist evolution, had intensified the distrust of the opposition. Nor did a Sukarno proposal early in 1957 that an Indonesian type of "guided democracy" (*demokrasi terpimpin*) or, to use the official term, "democracy with leadership," be instituted to replace the unsuitable western system stir any enthusiasm among the Sukarno opposition, either in the political parties or in the officers' corps.

Alarmed by growing communist strength on Java and increasingly disturbed over the seemingly disastrous drift of events, the Sukarno opposition, which includes some of the leading figures of the revolutionary leadership, in February, 1958, launched an ill-timed and ineptly-managed revolt, centering mostly on northern Sumatra and in the Christian areas of the Celebes. Although the Djakarta government acted with surprising speed and efficiency to reduce the revolt to isolated guerilla actions, it demonstrated again Indonesia's increasingly serious state of economic and political crisis.

In mid-1959 President Sukarno by emergency decree dissolved the slow-motion constituent assembly which had been engaged in drafting Indonesia's "permanent" constitution and reinstated the unitary constitution of 1945 as part of a not-too-successful campaign to revive the enthusiasm of the independence struggle. The following year saw the dissolution of the elected parliament, the postponement of scheduled elections, and the appointment of a so-called "mutual help" (*gotong-royong*) parliament divided between presidentially-favored political parties and "functional" groups. By mid-1961 the political oposition had been banned; and, with Sukarno ostensibly in control, Indonesia seemed embarked on a curious and unpredictable experiment in guided democracy and controlled economy. Coupled with this was a crusading effort on the part of its inscrutable, self-styled "voice of the revolution" to find a national soul at long last by an attempt to revive the emotions and reactions of the late 1940's. President Sukarno, who turned sixty in 1961, remained the unpredictable but the only key to what unity there was in Indonesia, supported by a curious and mutually distrustful coalition of Nationalists, Communists, vacillating Islamic conservatives (Nahdatul Ulama), and the Army command, each of which he skillfully and consistently balanced off against the other. What his departure might produce defies analysis since he has no adequate successor to control the political and social forces that since 1949 have seemed on the verge of destroying the nation.

Other than Indonesia, perhaps no area in Southeast Asia has experienced more travail and faces a more uncertain future than the former French empire on the Indo-Chinese peninsula. Until March, 1945, French Indo-China was technically the one European colonial possession which continued to be governed by its prewar rulers; for the local administration, giving allegiance to the Nazi-satellite Vichy regime of Marshal Pétain, was permitted by the Japanese to continue as the ostensible administration of the area. Unlike Burma or Indonesia during the first few years of Japanese occupation, the Vietnamese, possibly because of the traditional Sinic cultural links, seem to have given a minimum of cooperation—for that matter, less than the Vichy French officials gave. In May, 1941, Ho Chi Minh organized the Vietnam Independence League, better known to history as the Vietminh, the abbreviated form of its

Vietnamese name. From the beginning, the League followed the familiar pattern of nationalist united front movements, the Communists controlled the key positions. By early 1945, when the Japanese, increasingly distrustful of the French, finally took over direct control of Indo-China, the Vietminh controlled large areas in the Red River delta of the North. In September, following war's end, Ho proclaimed the Democratic Republic of Vietnam at Hanoi.

As in the case of the Indonesian travail, space does not permit any detailed discussion of the far more protracted agony through which Vietnam was forced to pass in the seven-and-one-half years between the outbreak of fighting between the Vietminh and the returning French forces in late 1946 and the Geneva accords of 1954. Early in 1946 it seemed that some sort of accord could be reached between the Vietminh, then apparently far more nationalist than communist oriented, and the new French Fourth Republic, which had jettisoned the old assimilation concept for de Gaulle's new idealistic vision of a "Union" of 100,000,000 Frenchmen.

But, just as they would attempt to do in Algeria fourteen years later, the military and the colonial groups in Indo-China sabotaged attempts at negotiation and sought to impose solution by armed force. For seven-and-one-half years, the French professional army, particularly its officer corps, was bled white in the jungles and the rice paddies of Indo-China, fighting against an elusive enemy that it could never force to fight in traditional fashion. Never, that is, until the Vietminh was ready to do so near the very end of the struggle; in May, 1954, it inflicted on the French at Dien Bien Phu perhaps the most sweeping and humiliating defeat suffered by any colonial power at the hands of "natives" since the Italian debacle at Adowa in 1896.

Military developments in Vietnam between 1946 and 1954 offered ample and depressing materials for study by western strategists struggling with the perplexing and ominous problems posed by the brushfire wars of the sixties. The outlines of the problem had already become clear with the Dutch failure to cope with a similar situation on Java between 1945 and 1949. Indo-China, at the expense of the French, grimly and completely filled in the details for all to note and ponder. In both cases, it was decisively demonstrated that the conduct of war by a modern army assumes (or, prior to the Dutch and French experiences, assumed) the existence of a certain psychological and technological infrastructure. It had been assumed a. that the enemy will stand and fight; b. that almost implicitly there will exist, à la Western Europe, a communications network suitable for use by trucks, tanks, and planes; c. that the side with superior firepower and logistics inevitably must win. In Indo-China, the Vietminh, after the Communist Chinese triumph of 1950, became increasingly well indoctrinated in Mao Tse Tung's dual concepts of guerilla and psychological warfare. Logistically they became stronger as supplies flowed across the Chinese border. This situation destroyed the traditional axioms of war. Coached by the Chinese, the Vietminh refused to fight a roadbound war where French equipment could function. Instead, they chose a tireless campaign of rice-paddy infiltration that exhausted the French potential and baffled its military command. And they used a masterful mixture of shrewd, culturally-oriented propaganda and of outright terrorism to assure support from the peasant population.

As early as 1948, the French sought to produce a psychological counter to Ho Chi Minh by utilizing the traditional symbolism of the Annamite emperors. They created a puppet State of Vietnam, headed by the last representative of the Nguyen dynasty, which had ruled Vietnam since the eighteenth century. Bao Dai, who had served the French and the Japanese as a compliant puppet, was a triumphant example of the French policy of assimilation. French-educated, speaking better French than Vietnamese, never happier than when at his Riviera villa, the portly, immaculately European-tailored Bao Dai was in sharp contrast with the frail "Father" Ho, who wore peasant clothes and looked like a village elder. Ironically, the complete success of the French policy of the gallicization of the ruling elites was also the measure of the failure of the Bao Dai experiment. Hampered both by French unwillingness to make concessions and by his own personal handicaps, Bao Dai was unable to offer any sort of counterappeal to the charisma of Ho.

French war weariness and international pressure led to the Geneva conference in the early summer of 1954, following the Dien Bien Phu debacle and American rejection of a final desperate French appeal for outright intervention. As a result of the conference, at which the roster of great power attendance showed the intensity of international involvement, Vietnam was partitioned (in theory, temporarily) at the seventeenth parallel into a Vietminh north and a non-communist but scarcely French-dominated south. Within two years of the Geneva conference, a plebiscite was to be held to settle the future destinies of both areas. At Hanoi, in the Red River delta of the north, Ho Chi Minh established the Democratic Republic of Vietnam (DRV) which rapidly assumed all the earmarks of a communist state, including in 1959 the adoption of a "socialist" constitution with Ho still continuing as "president."

In the south, the weakening French power in April, 1954, under heavy American pressure, had permitted Bao Dai in his role of Chief of State to appoint a new premier, Ngo Dinh Diem, an uncompromising, anti-French nationalist of aristocratic mandarin background, although a devout Catholic culturally as much a product of gallicization as Bao Dai himself. Given little initial prospects of survival, Diem quickly showed himself a strong and, at times, ruthless administrator who was able to win all-important American support, as the United States increasingly replaced France as the dominant power at Saigon. Backed by the United States as the only alternative to Ho, Diem within a year established effective control over the military forces and smashed the armed gangs of the religious sects, which the French had encouraged both as anti-communist forces and as wedges to split the nationalist movement. In October, 1955, Diem engineered a referendum to choose between himself and Bao Dai. Indorsed by a somewhat breathtaking 98 per cent majority, Diem proclaimed the Republic of Vietnam with himself as president while Bao Dai, presumably for the last time, returned to his Riviera villa.

As in the case of Indonesia, perhaps the highest praise that can be given to the Republic of Vietnam as of the early sixties is to note the mere fact of its survival. Its first weeks of existence were complicated by the tremendous torrent of refugees, estimated at 900,000, who came flooding down from the communist north. Internal security has constantly been a major problem as the Viet Cong (Vietminh) guerillas continue to operate in accelerating tempo. Backed by the U.S., Diem flatly refused in 1956 to hold the Geneva plebiscite and thus probably prevented what most observers had regarded as an inevitable communist victory.

By 1961 Diem had received close to two billion dollars in U.S. aid and, by all accounts, had achieved surprising economic stability in the traditionally rice surplus but industrially backward south. Successful resettlement of refugees, reconstruction of war-destroyed communications, increased agricultural production have all represented successes for the Diem regime. But, increasingly, experienced observers have been disturbed by what many see as the development of much the same characteristics that led the Chinese Nationalist regime down the road to defeat and to exile.

Although constitutionally Vietnam is a democratic republic, it has been a one-man state from the beginning. Never unsure of himself at any time, Diem increasingly seems to have acquired a sense of omniscience which, in a fashion reminiscent of Indonesia's Sukarno, equates opposition or even criticism with treason. Opposition parties have either joined the government or disappeared. As in Nationalist China, one party, the Revolutionary Personalism Party (Can Lao) which operates in a semi-secret fashion under the leadership of Diem's younger brother, Ngo Dinh Nhu, dominates the political scene. Although technically uncensored, the press operates in terms of "suggestions" from official sources within well understood, if unwritten, limits. April, 1961, saw Diem reelected by a 90 per cent majority against two carefully selected and unknown candidates. But the rising tide of communist guerilla infiltrations and a curiously confused and highly abortive revolt against the regime in November, 1960, by an elite paratroop regiment indicated that neither Diem, personally, nor his regime's policies had been able to create a stable anticommunist regime.

Attempts by the U.S. in mid-1961 to liberalize the regime fell on deaf ears, as had similar efforts in China in the late forties. Completing the Chinese parallel and very much in the Sinic tradition, was the family clique which dominated the destinies of Vietnam. Diem's brother, Ngo Dinh Nhu, officially Political Advisor to the President, is not only party boss but reportedly the "Sherman Adams" of the regime. Around his wife, again in the Kuomintang tradition, swirl rumors of palace intrigue and governmental corruption. Diem's three other brothers are respectively the Archbishop of Hue, ranking Catholic prelate; an important provincial governor; and the ambassador to London. Though drawing historical parallels may be dangerous, the Kuomintang-like trend of the Diem regime in the 1960's seemed to forebode disturbing possibilities, particularly in view of the mounting communist tide elsewhere in peninsular Southeast Asia.*

Nowhere was this more true than in the isolated landlocked little mountain kingdom of Laos which, until the early years of the sixties, when thought of at all, seemed to be an actual Shangri-La or, under its traditional designation as "the land of the thousand elephants," a fit setting for a

* By October, 1961, the Vietnamese situation had become serious enough for President Kennedy to send retired General Maxwell Taylor as his personal envoy to survey the situation. Although increased U.S. aid was pledged, the Kennedy administration was apparently reluctant to send U.S. troops except in terms of symbolic token support. There seemed little indication, however, that the Diem regime was either willing or able to check or reverse the reportedly mounting official corruption and sagging morale.

Gilbert and Sullivan operetta. It was not until 1949 that the French recognized the King of Luang Prabang as ruler over all of the multitribal approximately (1959) 2,000,000 population of the Laotian areas, which from time immemorial had been a buffer state or states between such powerful neighbors as Vietnam and Thailand. At the time of the Geneva accord, the two northern provinces of Laos were under the rule of the so-called Pathet Lao (Land of Lao) government, which under the leadership of Prince Souphanouvong, cousin to the king, was on terms of close ideological sympathy with Ho Chi Minh and the Vietminh. The Geneva truce commission in 1956 ruled for the incorporation of the Pathet Lao areas into Laos proper. But efforts to do this by a personal reconciliation between Souphanouvong and his older half-brother Souvanna Phouma (at various times prime minister and holder of other important posts) broke down in 1959 when clashes between Pathet Lao and royal troops took place, Vietminh guerilla infiltration intensified, and Prince Souphanouvong and some of his supporters were imprisoned on charges of treason. In May, 1960, he escaped and rejoined the Pathet Lao forces in the North.

Throughout 1959 and until August, 1960, the Royal Laotian Army continued to attempt unsuccessfully to wipe out the elusive Pathet Lao guerillas who were reportedly drawing on the experience of their Vietminh advisors and refused to fight in the traditional way for which the American-trained Laotian army was equipped. Since the Geneva accord, Laos has been the recipient of U.S. economic aid to the extent of over $300,000,000, the expenditure of a considerable portion of which has led to sweeping congressional investigation and censure. Since the Manila conference of September, 1954, when the Southeast Asia Treaty Organization (SEATO) was formed of which only two of eight members (Thailand and the Philippines) are Southeast Asian, Laos, Cambodia, and South Vietnam have been included under the protective umbrella of SEATO as obvious future targets for communist aggression.

In August, 1960, a coup by paratroops, more successful

in Laos than in Vietnam, under the leadership of Captain Kong Le, forced out the pro-American Government and installed Prince Souvanna Phouma as a neutralist pledged to stop the killing of Laotians by Laotians. The result, however, was to add yet a third dimension to civil strife. For almost immediately, army general Phoumi Nosavan launched an attack with his forces on the Souvanna Phouma regime and in December seized control of Laos's administrative capital of Vientiane. Souvanna Phouma fled across the Cambodian border, and Kong Le's forces retreated to the North where they linked up with the swelling forces of the Pathet Lao, now apparently receiving not only Vietminh but direct Soviet technical and logistic support. By mid-1961, Laos had become like Vietnam a major testing ground for Soviet and American influence. In March of that year the Soviet Union had agreed "in principle" to a cease-fire in Laos. The result was to prevent the much-rumored possibility of intervention either by the United States or the Southeast Asia Treaty Organization (SEATO). In May a fourteen nation conference on Laos convened for the first of a series of seemingly interminable sessions in Geneva. Geneva's record as a place of ill omen for so many of the idealistic international aspirations of the twentieth century seemed unlikely to be changed by the Laotian conference. For by the time the conference's first meeting took place, continued Pathet Lao offensives had placed at least half of Laos's 90,000 square miles under communist control instead of the approximate one fourth which the Pathet Lao had dominated at the time of the Soviet "in principle" agreement to the cease-fire.

Aside from the world powers concerned, three Laotian groups were involved at Geneva. Backed by the U.S. was the official Laotian delegation, appointed by Premier Prince Boun Oum whom General Phoumi Nosavan had placed in power following his December, 1960, victory over the neutralist forces of Captain Kong Le and Prince Souvanna Phouma, whom Moscow and Peking recognized as premier. The third Laotian delegation at the conference was that of Prince Souphanouvong, Souvanna Phouma's younger half-brother, whose leftist Neo Lao Hak Xat party received the military support of the openly pro-communist Pathet Lao.

After interminable discussions both in Geneva and in Laos itself, the three princes announced agreement "in principle" early in October, 1961, to form a so-called compromise regime with neutralist Prince Souvanna Phouma as premier. But it was not until mid-June, 1962, that the haggling over cabinet posts finally came to an end and the new regime was able to take office. Initially, the failure to reach agreement on the division of cabinet posts in the proposed coalition had been caused by the intransigent attitude taken by the two leaders of the previously American-backed official regime, Prince Boun Oum and his military protector, General Phoumi Nosavan. Understandably they had been reluctant to see such key posts as the premiership and the defense and interior ministries surrendered to followers of Prince Souvanna Phouma who, in spite of his technically neutral political status, is regarded as very much under the influence of his communist half-brother, Prince Souvanouvong. In spite of heavy American pressure, including the suspension in February, 1962, of monthly subsidies in excess of $3,000,000, General Nosavan and Prince Boun Oum had resisted giving way to the projected coalition regime up to the very end, even attempting to recruit support for their position from Thailand, South Vietnam, and Nationalist China.

As of early May in northern Laos, the cease-fire between the Boun Oum regime and the Pathet Lao came to an abrupt end. The responsibility for this is difficult to determine. It seems not unlikely that the cease-fire violation may have been deliberately provoked as a last desperate gamble by the government to force outright American intervention and the abandonment of support for the coalition regime. Although the United States did dispatch some 5,000 troops to Thailand, American support for the dubious experiment of the proposed coalition remained unchanged and, after an almost routine last minute "hesitation waltz" on the part of the three princes, the coalition regime took office in late June. Immediately it was very clear where the real center of its power lay. Prince Boun Oum announced his retirement from political life and, in terms reminiscent of Bao Dai, Prince Souvanna Phouma immediately left his native land for a stay of unannounced duration in the far more attractive atmosphere of France. It was clearly with no reluctance that Prince Souvanouvong and his followers prepared to take over effective control of government. Of the nineteen cabinet seats involved, eleven are occupied by so-called neutralists, with four each for the outright communist and the pro-Western groups.

In spite of the obviously predestined failure to achieve a genuinely neutralist regime in Laos, the State Department seemed unable or unwilling to formulate any consistent or coherent approach to the political problems of Southeast Asia as had so obviously governed the communist approach to the area. Fragmented confusion seemed unhappily to be the term most descriptive of American activity in the area. In South Vietnam there was increasingly active involvement; in Thailand the manifestation of the American "presence"; in Laos a seemingly deliberate refusal to face the fact that whatever meager chances of success the coalition regime concept had ever had were long since vanished. It appeared not unlikely, as had been the case so many times before, that the State Department with a wary eye cocked on domestic opinion was continuing to give lip service to a policy that it was well aware had already failed.

For, as of mid-1962, there seemed little question but that Laos, as slowly but inevitably as the crumbling away of an already flood-weakened levee, was destined to become the new high watermark in the floodtide of communism's advance in Southeast Asia. The result, short of outright American intervention in force, makes the survival of a non-communist regime in South Vietnam an increasingly dubious prospect. Nor does it seem unlikely that a regime so acutely attuned to survival as that of Thailand will fail to understand and act upon the conclusions to be drawn from Laotian developments. For that matter, any re-orientation of policy by the remaining non-communist states of mainland Southeast Asia is likely to be led off by Prince Norodom Sihanouk, formerly king and now, by his own choice, Head of State of Cambodia, who until now has been the area's most financially and psychologically successful practicioner of neutral neutralism.

Since the Khmer empire, which dominated most of peninsular Southeast Asia at the time of the Fourth Crusade and left behind it the magnificence of Angkor Wat and Angkor Thom, Cambodia has lived the perilous existence of all small and weak states trapped by geography between powerful and expansion-minded neighbors. Faced as always with the traditional threat of Thailand from the west and of Vietnam from the east, it must have been with a sense of relief that the reigning monarch of the time welcomed a French protectorate in 1863.

Like the swamp reed of a Japanese emperor's New Year's poem, Cambodia bowed to the tempests of World War II and escaped unharmed. And during the tragic years between 1946 and 1954, it was not much involved in the destructive events that took such toll in Vietnam itself. Indeed, that special providence which Lord Bryce described as guarding the destiny of the United States seems to be equally concerned with Cambodia, passively since the beginning of the French protectorate and actively since Cambodia was forced by the Geneva conference to make its sovereign way in the world.

For that matter, supporters of the great-man theory of history—even royalists disheartened by the twentieth century—could find much to cheer them in the person of Prince Norodom Sihanouk, king from 1941 to 1955; he alone is responsible for the good fortune by which until now Cambodia has survived under the incessant challenges of the modern world. As has no other Southeast Asian leader, Sihanouk, another product of French education, has made neutralism pay off. He is apparently blessed with an intuitive comprehension of power politics in the mid-twentieth century, for his neutral neutralism has made a virtue of the necessity faced by his Georgia-sized, 5,000,-

000 population, nation. Cambodia as an adherent to either big power bloc would count for little. But Cambodia as an uncommited neutral in an as yet undecided area of the world offers a marketplace in which competing nations and ideologies can hawk their wares.

The result, as a distinguished American authority on Southeast Asia, Dr. Willard Hanna of the American Universities Field Service, noted in 1960, was that Cambodia's 400,000 population capital of Phnom-Penh could boast as of that date the following: a. an American 100-bed hospital for Buddhist priests; b. a $12,500,000 163-bed French hospital for general use, plus an ultra-modern 500-student school, plus a $2,500,000 airport; c. a Soviet-built 500-bed "gift" hospital calculated to surpass that of the French; d. a communist-Chinese-donated-and-installed 20-kilowatt radio station for the Information Ministry, which also profits from the facilities of an American-donated modern printing plant; e. a 140-mile $32,000,000 modern "Road of Khmer-American Friendship" which connects the capital with the $10,000,000 French-constructed new seaport of Sihanoukville, intended to reduce Cambodia's dependence on South Vietnamese sea connections; f. other various multi-national projects, including a Mekong River "T.V.A." Project, sponsored by the U.N. and intended to benefit not only Cambodia but the other riverine countries of the area.

In 1955, reportedly because of his belief that a more active role was necessary, Sihanouk abdicated as king in favor of his father to become prime minister and leader of his own personally created Popular Socialist Community Party. Sihanouk's philosophy of international politics was perhaps best summarized by his penetrating observation, "The interplay of American and Communist influence is what really makes Cambodian independence possible." How much longer, in the atmosphere of mounting crisis of the present, Sihanouk can continue to lead his nation across a frayed tightrope over the threatening gulf below remains to be seen. But past experience would seem to argue that he probably can continue to do so longer and more effectively than anyone else, or at least that he can continue to do so until the influence of one or the other of the great world blocs becomes so predominant in Southeast Asia as to exclude the possibility of turning to the other as a balancing force—a development that seems unlikely in the foreseeable future. Following his father's death in 1959, Sihanouk's political acuteness was again demonstrated when, following a nation-wide referendum which endorsed his policies by 2,020,000 votes out of 2,020,349 cast, he assumed the far more flexible title of Head of State rather than strait-jacketing himself into the restricting traditional isolation of the monarchy. A Head of State, of course, can continue in office regardless of whether the strength of the prevailing political winds dictates bowing to East or West.*

The most peaceful and orderly transitions from colonial to independent status of the larger areas of Southeast Asia have been those of the Philippine Republic and of the Federation of Malaya, unique as the world's only elective monarchy. In spite of the tremendous devastation of the war years, the Commonwealth of the Philippines became an independent nation on July 4, 1946, as was promised twelve years earlier. In its independent existence as in its colonial history, the Philippines has continued to go its separate way in Southeast Asia. Between it and the United States there was no bitter gulf as in the French and in the Dutch situations. There were rather the shared memories of Bataan and Corregidor, of mutual sacrifice and mutual victory. Prior to the transfer of independence, the election campaign to choose the first president resulted in a victory for Manuel Roxas of the newly-formed Liberal Party, which now displaced the Nationalists who dominated the Commonwealth period (1935-1941 actually, although the Commonwealth was recognized by the U.S. and

* By the end of October, 1961, Sihanouk, after severing diplomatic ties with Thailand earlier in the month, was publicly discussing the desirability of severing all ties with the Western powers in view of the trend of Southeast Asian developments.

the other allies as the legal government during the Japanese period also).

Relations with the U.S., particularly centering around economic problems, reconstruction, and internal security, were the major problems with which the new Philippine government was forced to cope. American rehabilitation aid was tied to Philippine acceptance of the Bell Trade Act of 1946 which required equal rights for exploitation by American and Philippine citizens of Philippine natural resources until 1974. Under the pressure of dire necessity, approval of the provision was jammed through the Philippine congress and approved by a constitutional amendment on which 60 per cent of Philippine citizens declined to vote. The resentment aroused by the whole course of events connected with the Bell Act left a pall of bitterness for some years thereafter over the other problems which have arisen in the contacts between the two nations.

The torrent of American aid poured into the Philippines in the form of emergency loans, tax refunds, war damage claims, and rehabilitation amounted to approximately two billion dollars within a five year period. The personal opportunities it offered for enrichment proved too much for most government officials. It will be remembered that the rapid "Filipinization" of the civil service in the first years of the American occupation had offered too limited a period to bring about much change in the standards of public morality inherited from the Spanish period or in the traditional concepts of obligation for family welfare. In the period of the late forties the shortcomings of this policy became glaringly clear.

Not only did considerable sums stick to the fingers of those supposed to disburse them, but the great landowners were the major beneficiaries of the rehabilitation funds; further, little was done to implement the long-needed land reforms which already in central Luzon had brought about abortive peasant revolts in the interwar period. Peasant resentment in the period of the late forties found adequate expression in the existence of the Hukbalahaps (Peoples' Army Against the Japanese) which, like the

Vietminh, had been formed as early as 1942 as a predominantly patriotic nationalist front against the Japanese but with strong communist flavoring in the leadership. After various fruitless efforts on the part of President Roxas and his successor Quirino at sporadic negotiations and equally sporadic efforts at armed suppression, the situation in the rich agricultural areas of Luzon became increasingly worse. It seemed that the "Peoples' Liberation Army," as the Huks under the leadership of self-proclaimed communist Luis Taruc now called themselves, might well match the triumphs of the Vietminh.

Until 1950 there was little evidence, either political or economic to rebut this. The process of bribery and violence by which Quirino's Liberals had carried the 1949 presidential election marked a new nadir in mockery of democratic processes. Economically, the profligate mismanagement of the U.S. aid funds had created domestic inflation and acute governmental cash shortages with commitments unmet and salaries unpaid at the same time that a drop in world copra prices deprived the virtually bankrupt nation of urgently needed foreign exchange.

Through the Philippine-requested Bell Economic Survey Mission, the U.S. and the Philippines reached agreement in November, 1950, that in conjunction with land and tax reform, plus other economic legislation, a loan in the amount of $250,000,000 would be extended over a five year period. At approximately the same time, a young ex-guerilla congressman, Ramon Magsaysay, was appointed Secretary of Defense to reform the Army and to resolve the Huk problem. By 1953 Magsaysay was on the way to becoming the most promising and dynamic figure of the postwar period. Possessed of tremendous energy, a Roosevelt-like distaste for administrative details, understanding of the common man's problems, and an ability to project himself to crowds reminiscent of both Franklin Roosevelt and Wendell Willkie, Magsaysay by a combination of military force, understanding of the peasant's problems, and a hard-pushed land reform campaign contained the Huk threat and became obvious presidential timber.

With much the same eager desperation that Eisenhower had been seized on by the professional politicians a year earlier, the office-hungry Nationalists made Magsaysay their candidate in the 1953 election. After an unprecedented barnstorming type of campaign which drew uniquely wide interest and, for the first time in the Philippines, support from a nationwide non-party group of young middle-class citizens, Magsaysay was swept into the presidency with the new record participation of 78 per cent of the voters, whose keen interest and voluntary pollwatching kept the traditional use of fraud and intimidation to a bare minimum. In his three years of office, before a fatal plane accident in March, 1957, Magsaysay served his nation well.

It is arguable that Magsaysay had not been able to achieve the pledged "impossible" of his 1953 election campaign. Yet in the brief span given him, his tangible as well as intangible achievements and his new beginnings seemed to mark a new era in Philippine political life. For Americans there was a New Deal first-hundred-days atmosphere about Magsaysay's administration—in its achievements, its beginnings, its atmosphere, and even in its disappointments. Integrity and honest work were demanded from the civil service; land reform and peasant credit projects were initiated; highway programs to help the peasant in marketing his crop were undertaken; with the capture of Huk leader Taruc, security was restored; above all, the presidential palace, in the words of Magsaysay's successors, became "the palace of the people." The Philippine masses were given a sense of direct and immediate rapport with government. Magsaysay introduced a new concept of the relationship between rulers and ruled, never before experienced in Southeast Asia. However abortive his reforms, he left an unforgettable imprint on his nation's political process.

The vote which made Magsaysay's Vice-President, Carlos Garcia, president after the 1957 election was a minority choice from among a unique four-candidate selection which also saw the vice-presidency captured by the Liberal

Party's Diosdado Macapagal with 117,000 more votes than Garcia had received for the presidency. During the campaign and throughout the four years of the Garcia administration it seemed that the sticky-fingered, pre-Magsaysay philosophy of political morality had reasserted itself.

Vice-President Macapagal, nominated by the underdog Liberals, made the corruption and maladministration of the Garcia administration the chief issue of a violence-ridden election campaign which was expected to confirm Garcia in the presidency. But with Magsaysay-like enthusiasm and thoroughness, Macapagal barnstormed the Philippines carrying to the voters in the remotest barrios his pledge to bring back "decency and prosperity." Whether because of his pledge to accept "command responsibility" for whatever graft or maladministration might occur or because of his emphasis on his own poverty-stricken boyhood, Macapagal emerged the surprise victor with a 600,000 vote plurality over Garcia, his only other opponent. The election itself, in contrast to the campaign, took place without violence and seemed to indicate an increasing degree of political maturity which augured well for the continued growth of constitutional democracy in the Philippines.

None of the new nations of Southeast Asia has been privileged to embark on its independent course with more dignity or careful planning than the Federation of Malaya, whose sovereign status was proclaimed to the world on August 31, 1957. Behind the proclamation was more than a decade of constitutional drafting and redrafting and hours of discussion between Great Britain, the nine Malayan princely rulers, and the representatives of Malayan, Chinese and Indian political groups. While all this had been slowly but majestically progressing, Malaya, on the pattern of the Vietminh and of the Hukbalahaps, had known the costly destruction in lives and property of a virulent communist-terrorist guerilla campaign launched in 1948 by the so-called Malayan Races Liberation Army, although from the beginning until July 31, 1960, the officially proclaimed end of the "Emergency," the MRLA was almost entirely Chinese in composition and support.

Under the sympathetic and perceptive guidance of Governor-General Malcolm MacDonald, who probably has made a more meaningful mark on colonial history than his late father on domestic political history, the prototype for the political organization of independent Malaya was brought into existence as early as February 1, 1948, with the inauguration of a Federation of Malaya. Under a single effective administrative apparatus headed by a High Commissioner, the nine sultanates and the settlements of Francis Light's Penang and history-burdened Malacca were grouped together for the first time. Outside this eleven-unit federation was Singapore, organized as a separate Crown colony. Within the federation, it was possible to have either British nationality or that of any one of the nine Malay states. It was from this initial constitutional basis that nine years later there emerged the shape of the not so different independent Malayan federation and of the pre-World War I "dominion" status city state of Singapore.

Aside from the strains imposed by the Emergency, the period between federation and independence—in spite of occasional hesitations and stumblings—was one of general progress in all fields. The prewar excellence of the Malayan Civil Service (modelled on the famed Indian Civil Service) was reconstructed, while social welfare and economic development programs were carried out. Economically and inescapably it seemed, Malaya's Achilles's heel continued to be its dependence on the two export commodities of rubber and tin which accounted for 25 per cent of the gross national product and, at times, as much as 85 per cent of the export trade. In particular, these important exports were dependent on the fluctuations of the American market, which made them unstable, if highly important, revenue sources.

By mid-1955 the first elections were held for an expanded Federal Legislative Council with the electoral system based on the characteristic Anglo-American arrangement of single member districts and victory secured by simple majority. Of the estimated 1,600,000 Federation citizens eligible, approximately 1,250,000 registered, and more than 1,000,000 actually voted. The election marked an important development in Malayan political evolution. For, dominating the election campaign as the only group putting up candidates for all of the fifty-two seats at stake, and then capturing all but one, along with 84 per cent of the vote, was the Malay-Chinese-Indian-Alliance (MCIA), embodying a bold and surprisingly successful attempt to break through the communal isolation which had so fragmented and paralyzed political action until that time.

Grudgingly, slowly, and warily the United Malays National Organization (UMNO), which had become the dominant party for the Malay population, and the Malayan Chinese Association (MCA) had joined forces as early as 1952 to offer a joint ticket for the Kuala Lumpur municipal elections. The success of this venture led the Alliance to continue as it soon became clear—in spite of official British coolness—that the only hopeful basis for cooperation between the races in Malaya lay in a frank recognition of communal differences rather than in trying to achieve the cultural fusion envisaged by the British authorities. By the time of the 1955 election, the original big two of the Alliance were joined by the Malayan Indian Congress (MIC), the chief spokesman for the (1957 census) 700,000 Indians resident in the Malay states.

By February, 1956, the Malayan Federation Constitutional Conference, meeting in London, had agreed to the transfer of power with August 31, 1957, as the target date. The drafting of the proposed constitution was entrusted to a distinguished international commission of jurists which produced a 181 paragraph constitution; it provides a fascinating summary of the accumulated constitutional experience of the modern world, particularly the Anglo-American. The constitution outlined a conventional type of parliamentary system but contained the unique feature of an elective king as the chief of state. The Yang di-Pertuan Agung is chosen for a five-year term from among themselves by the nine Malayan rulers.

Since independence, Malaya has chosen to remain with

the Commonwealth of Nations; and, although tensions have not been absent, the Alliance, contrary to various gloomy predictions, has held together. When the first elections to the Malayan House of Representatives were held in 1959, the Alliance won seventy of the one hundred seats at stake with the other thirty divided among five parties and three independents. Of the other parties, only the Pan-Malayan Islamic Party, advocating an ethnic Malay nationalism and closer ties with Indonesia, made even a noticeable showing by electing thirteen members. "The PMIP," writes Dr. Willard Hanna in an American Universities Field Service Report of mid-1960, "bubbles up a strange brew of Islamic conservatism and intolerance, Marxist idealism and dogma, anti-Western, anti-Chinese, anti-Alliance, and pro-Indonesian attitudes."

But in spite of the eagerness of the PMIP to exploit racial cleavages within the Alliance and of the efforts of the Socialists to capitalize on discontent with the Government's conservative economic policies, Prime Minister Abdul Rahman, in the early 1960's, continued to drive his political troika with a light but firm hand. Given Malaya's apparent, if at times too nicely-balanced, political, economic, and social stability, the new nation seemed justified in viewing its future prospects with optimism—even though few impartial observers were ready to accept at face value the Prime Minister's 1960 statement of his intent to devote his major attention thenceforth to foreign affairs, since all domestic problems were so completely under control.

Singapore, separated from the rest of Malaya as early as 1946, formally achieved full internal self-government as of June, 1959. Its constitutional status is reminiscent of that enjoyed by the self-governing dominions in the period before the First World War. The governmental structure comprises a prime minister, responsible to the unicameral legislative assembly, a ceremonial supreme head of state who must be of Malay descent, and the British resident Commissioner for Singapore, also Commissioner-General for Southeast Asia, who has responsibility for defense and for foreign affairs other than those concerned with cultural and commercial interests.

Relations between Singapore and the Federation have been those of the eager suitor and the reluctant lady. In Malaya itself, the Malays number even now a bare 50 per cent of the total population. If Singapore were included within Federation boundaries, its 76 per cent Chinese population (of a total one-and-one-half million) would reduce the Malay percentage in the enlarged Federation to 41 per cent and raise the Chinese from the present 37 per cent to a dominant 44 per cent. (The difference would be made up principally by the Indian-Pakistan minorities, presently 11 per cent of Malaya's population and 8.5 per cent of Singapore's.)

Singapore's political history in the decade prior to 1959 is the story of the growing political importance and increasingly leftward slant of the Chinese community, which had already achieved economic and numerical predominance. Since 1948, when Singapore held its first election, registered voters have increased from 35,000 to a virtually complete adult suffrage of 690,000 in 1959, of whom 530,-000 voted in the May legislative assembly elections of that year. The number of legislative members popularly elected has kept pace with the steady widening of the franchise, increasing from six out of twenty-three in 1948 to the entire body of fifty-one legislators in 1959.

Of the fifty-one legislators chosen in the "independence" election of 1959, forty-three were members of the Peoples' Action Party. The PAP is iconoclastically and, at times, erratically leftwing Marxist in its orientation, largely Chinese-supported, although it apparently has some Malay support as well. The party was organized in 1954 by a brilliant young British-educated Chinese from a well-to-do merchant family. Lee Kuan Yew, in terms both of his political interest and of his leftist orientation, personified the change that had taken place beween his own generation and the traditionally apolitical "economic man" outlook of his father's contemporaries who, when they did concern themselves with political affairs, were almost instinctively in favor of the status quo.

Since its 1959 election victory, the PAP seems to have been sobered by the responsibilities of power and by the realization of the importance of the maintenance of commercial and business reliability to Singapore's future. A new chapter was opened in the political history of the Malayan peninsula when, following a two-day conference in late September, 1961, Lee Kuan Yew and Prime Minister Tengku Abdul Rahman announced formal plans for the merging of Singapore and the Malayan Federation by June, 1963. Under the tentative merger plans, the Malayan Federation will accept responsibility for Singapore's defense and security but Singapore will retain independent jurisdiction over labor and education. Although the problem of the SEATO base at Singapore remained unsettled, British approval of the merger plans in late November, 1961, seemed to clear the way for their completion.

An even more ambitious merger was suggested for all the present and former British colonial areas of Southeast Asia by Prime Minister Tengku Abdul Rahman in May, 1961. Under the proposed plan a "Greater Malaysia Union," presumably on a federated basis, would be created with its constituent units composed of Malaya, Singapore, the Crown colonies of North Borneo and Sarawak—both now moving towards self-government—and the British-protected sultanate of tiny (2200 square miles) but oil-rich Brunei. Brunei, for much the same reasons that led Jamaica to withdraw from the proposed West Indies Federation, has been suspicious of any political merger with its immediate neighbors because of the financial aspects but the inclusion of Malaya and Singapore may help to erase these reservations. In October, 1961, the Malayan parliament passed a resolution approving the plan.

3

THE MAJOR PROBLEMS
OF CONTEMPORARY
SOUTHEAST ASIA

1. Introduction

In this concluding section we shall examine briefly the more important problems which confront contemporary Southeast Asia. In varying degrees they are common to all the new nations of the area, although their importance naturally varies from one country to another. For example, the minorities problem continues to be a potential threat to the very existence of Burma and Indonesia. But in Thailand, except for the uncertain allegiance of the Chinese population, and in Vietnam, there is no serious minority problem. Indonesia is still searching for a meaningful national identity, while Malaya and the Philippines, on the other hand, offer instances of institutional stability which seem likely to continue indefinitely.

The choice of major problems common to so diverse a group of nations is, of course, rather arbitrary and there would undoubtedly be considerable variation among any group of informed students. Indeed, considering the wide fluctuation in degrees of importance from one country to another, it would be absurd to attempt to make any evaluation of relative importance in terms of Southeast Asia at large. The sequence in which they are presented does, however, have significance. It is an effort in terms of dynamic flow and causal relationships to indicate the connection between the various problems rather than to view each one separately as a uniquely isolated situation, meaninglessly torn out of the "ecology" which gives it a related significance. In terms of this flow sequence, the first problem we shall consider is that of governmental institutions which for several of Southeast Asia's new nations remains an unsolved and troubling priority item on the national agenda.

2. Governmental Institutions

As in the pre-European period, the constitutions of contemporary Southeast Asia bear witness to the powerful influences exerted by the non-indigenous political forces currently dominant in the area. Without exception, including the Democratic Republic of Vietnam, this is true for all of Southeast Asia from Laos to the Philippines. One of the most obvious of requisite status symbols for acceptance as respectable members of the world community was the adoption of a western-type governmental system by each of the new nations as it emerged from colonialism. Indeed, involved in this was a certain element of "homeopathic magic" (Frazer, *The Golden Bough,* Ch. III) based on the concept that "like produces like." If the governmental systems of Great Britain, France, the Netherlands, and the United States had enabled these nations to become great and powerful, then let us go and do likewise. The hallmark of being a modern and progressive nation was to have a carefully spelled-out system of parliamentary representation with proper lip service given to the concept of elections and pious genuflections made to the most modern concepts of the political and social rights of the individual citizens.

The result, while often producing documents that were impeccable in their drafting and in the nobility of their intentions, was to create constitutions that were little more than promissory notes on the future—a future which under optimum conditions is improbable in Southeast Asia for many decades. These "model" constitutions have had little meaning for the citizens who lived under them. In the

Southeast Asian tradition, it is a case of elite and mass each functioning within its own but seldom-intersecting world. For the villager in his rice paddy, votes of confidence and the feverish game of cabinet musical chairs played by the governing elite in the far-distant capital are as remote and meaningless as had been for his ancestors the intrigues of the aristocracy around the thrones of the sacred god-kings.*

In the first hopeful dawn of independence, leaders of the new nations indulged in much romanticizing about the indigenous democratic traditions present in their countries. Usually this was embellished with references to the village councils and other such "democratic" instances. But of the tremendous gap between these classic concepts and modern twentieth century democracy, nothing was ever said, if indeed realized. Between the status democracy of the remote past, insofar as it ever existed, and the twentieth-century concept of egalitarianism, no link can be found nor rapport be expected. Western governmental institutions, produced by a totally alien cultural and social heritage, have proved inappropriate to the psychological and political needs of most of Southeast Asia. To this statement must be noted the exceptions of the Philippines and Malaya. The Philippines, as we have noted earlier, conforms far more to a Latin than to a Southeast Asian pattern, although here too as in most of Latin America the functioning of the governmental system bears not too close a resemblance to its prototype. In the case of Malaya, although the period of independence is still very brief, it would seem that the happy combination of thorough British tutelage, highly competent local leadership, and economic well-being augur well for the successful operation of the truly model Malayan constitution.

Elsewhere in Southeast Asia, indeed elsewhere in the

* For a comprehensive and highly interesting discussion of the problems involved, see Edward Shils' "Political Developments in the New States," *Comparative Studies in Society and History, An International Quarterly,* II, 3, 4 (April, 1960; July, 1960), 265-292; 379-411.

Afro-Asian world from Ghana to Korea, the situation is quite otherwise. Typical has been the indifference to western-type institutions by the masses; their sometimes cynical manipulation by the ruling elite*; failure of the constitutional promissory notes ever to mature; growing political and social disillusionment; and in Thailand, Egypt, Indonesia, Burma, Pakistan, Sudan, Iraq, Turkey, and Korea, the abolition or suspension of "democratic institutions" by a charismatic leader or by the army as the one stable apolitical authority available to "save" the nation. From the moment of its birth, South Vietnam under Ngo Dinh Diem has resembled nothing so much as a Confucian-based mandarinate with little attention paid to either letter or spirit of its western-type constitution modelled, like the Philippines', on an American prototype. By presidential decree, Indonesia in 1959, abandoned its third constitution and returned to the original independence document of 1945. This, accompanied by frenzied exhortations from Indonesia's President Sukarno for "a return to the spirit of '45," was as much an invocation of "homeopathic magic" as were any of the earlier constitutional ventures. In terms of so-called "guided democracy," Sukarno has led his nation in a so far fruitless search to find suitable alternatives to western-style liberal "free for all" economy and the equally objectionable "outmoded" concepts of "liberal, Western-style democracy." North Vietnam has operated as a typical totalitarian satellite state from the moment of its inception in 1954 while Laos, in spite of the constitutional monarchy formally established in 1947, has uniquely personified the ideological conflicts of the Cold War in terms of traditional princely political maneuverings. Again, in the case of Cambodia the contrast is obvious between the

* In many instances, it seems probable that no deliberate "cynical manipulation" was involved but merely that traditional and customary political, or rather social, habit patterns were almost unconsciously followed. There is an obvious and painful dichotomy involved in the contrast between the Anglo-American concept of "public office as a public trust" and the traditional Asian moral responsibility to provide for the less economically fortunate members of one's family clan.

theory of its constitutional structure and its complete domination by Prince Norodom Sihanouk who operates far less
on the basis of inherited right than as a twentieth-century
political leader.

It seems demonstrable that few—and not even these
completely—of the nations of Southeast Asia are prepared
any longer to fabricate their governmental structures in
terms of western constitutional prototypes. The political
developments of the last decade offer convincing proof
that most of the new nations have come into existence
sadly lacking in the basic social, cultural, economic, administrative, and political infrastructure without which a western-type constitutional democracy cannot function. On the
other hand, drawing on the evidence of the past decade, it
seems clear that, except as a last resort of despair and
disillusionment, no new nation is going to embrace the
communist totalitarian alternative. Whether there is still
time for an indigenous synthesis, possibly in terms of a
democratically based social welfare state to emerge, is very
much a question.

To expect popular participation, as understood in the
Anglo-American sense, in Southeast Asian governmental
activities for decades to come is to indulge in wishful thinking. Again the Philippines and possibly Malaya may well
prove exceptions to this. Aside from North Vietnam, the
leaders of modern Southeast Asia all talk in terms of constitutional governmental systems, either as alleged actuality
or a desirable goal. In governmental as in other areas
an attempt must be made to judge Southeast Asia's achievements and possibilities in terms of indigenous values—not
those of an alien culture produced by a quite different
heritage.

It would seem that the most realistic course for Southeast
Asian constitutional evolution to follow would be along the
lines of Sukarno's attempt to formulate a concept of "guided
democracy" or along the far more coherent plan of Ayub
Khan for "basic democracies." In this connection, the
present leaders of Southeast Asia might find much food for
thought in the series of lectures (especially lecture 5)

delivered almost forty years ago by the first of modern Asia's great nationalist leaders, Dr. Sun Yat Sen, on the general topic of "Democracy"—the second of the three principles which in his *San Min Chu I* he outlined to his countrymen as their guides into the modern world. Summarizing the type of tutelage democracy necessary for the China of the mid-twenties, Sun told his fellow-nationalists, ". . . we must distinguish between sovereignty and ability. The foundations of the government of a nation must be built upon the rights of the people, but the administration of government must be entrusted to experts." Unheeded as his advice was by the subsequent leadership of the Kuomintang, it would seem highly relevant to contemporary Southeast Asia.

Barring world catastrophe, the next decade may see all the nations of Southeast Asia—with the probable exception of North Vietnam—making progress in their task of achieving meaningful intra-national consensus on governmental structure and constitutional organization. In terms of classic liberal economic and political theory, the results may not be altogether pleasing to western observers. For that matter, Peking and Moscow commentators may also find little difficulty in restraining their enthusiasm. Important in this task will be the motivating ideologies, to which we now turn. One further observation must be noted, however. If the present leadership of Southeast Asia or a competent non-communist alternative, possibly drawn from army sources, is unable to convince the people that they are capable of coping with the crucial problems of the present, then Peking may well within the next decade be exercising sway over a ring of satellite states beyond the most ambitious expansionist dreams of the Ming emperors.

3. Ideologies

In the decade of the fifties, one could make the loose and rather inaccurate generalization that, avowed communists aside, the leaders of Southeast Asia were Jeffersonian democrats in their political outlook and Marxists in their economic thinking—Marxists that is to the extent that virtually without exception they accepted the axiomatic nature of Lenin's equation of imperialism and colonialism with western capitalism, which therefore was automatically "bad" and an influence to be guarded against with vigilant suspicion. A social welfare state was a basic point in the various nationalist programs. Nor was the Marxist concept of public ownership of basic industries a jarring one. Both in the pre-colonial period and—particularly in the Netherlands Indies—during the colonial period, state control and monopoly of important aspects of economic life had been widespread.

The Soviet and the Chinese experiences have undoubtedly had considerable impact on even the most avowedly anti-communist nations in contemporary Southeast Asia. The Soviet Union has always benefited from its identification as the prime example of a former backward peasant nation which has successfully achieved these social welfare goals along with economic maturity precisely because of its emphatic rejection of western capitalism and acceptance of social and economic planning. As a brilliant American scholar has recently observed (Adam B. Ulam, *The Unfinished Revolution,* New York, 1960), Marxism is uniquely appealing for societies involved in the painful transition from agricultural to industrial or industrializing economies. Given the initial advantages enjoyed by Marxism and the pressing urgency of Southeast Asia's social and economic problems, it is a tribute both to the power of indigenous social and cultural influences and to the realism of current leadership that its impact has found expression in the broad eclecticism of the social welfare state rather than in rigidly prescribed doctrinal programs.

The ideological viewpoints of Southeast Asia's ruling groups range all the way from the undeviating Leninist-Maoist party line of North Vietnam to the profoundly unideological American-type pragmatism of the Philippines. While it can be said that nationalism is an important factor everywhere, this is still of very little help in clarifying the important differences among the highly dynamic socialist nationalism* of Indonesia, the adaptable and rather passive nationalism of Thailand, and the use made of it as an ideological weapon by the Vietminh. Separated from its linkage with anti-colonialism which gave it such dynamic if destructive force during the period of the independence struggles, it seems questionable as to whether nationalism can play an integrating, constructive role in the new nations.

The role of religion in modern Southeast Asia is significant. In two instances at least, the Sarikat Islam of Indonesia and the Buddhist Young Men's Association of Burma, it inspired the development of the nationalist movements. In contrast to the secularism of modern western nationalism, religious revivals have been an important aspect in the development of the area. The stress laid on Buddhism in Burma and in Thailand is well known, and in Indonesia much of political history since independence has been concerned with the clash between Islam as an ideological focus and Javanese mystical nationalism inspired by traditional Hindu-Buddhist foundations.

Five principles, the *Pantjasila,* first outlined by Sukarno in 1945 as Indonesia's official philosophy, offer perhaps the best example of the varied sources on which Southeast Asia's ruling elite has drawn in an effort to create a meaningful synthesis. Before the Japanese-sponsored Preparatory Committee for Indonesian Independence in June, 1945, Sukarno outlined the philosophical basis on which the prospective Indonesian state should be founded. The basic principles involved were these: 1. Nationalism; 2. Internationalism; 3. Representative Government; 4. Social Prosperity; 5. Belief in God. In the course of his address, Sukarno quoted widely from such varied sources as Sun Yat Sen, Lenin, John Reed, Ernest Renan, Otto Bauer, Jean Jaurès, geopolitics, Islamic religious principles, Japanese experience, and Javanese tradition. Indeed, he concluded by condensing the basic meaning of his five prin-

---

* In its economic orientation, Indonesian nationalism, as expressed in the programs of both the religious and secular parties, has always had a strong "socialist" orientation.

ciples in traditional Javanese terms saying, "If I compress what was five to get three, and what was three to get one, then I have a genuine Indonesian term, the term 'gotong royong' (mutual cooperation). The State of Indonesia, which we are going to establish, should be a state of mutual cooperation. How fine that is! A Gotong Royong state!"

Just as the concepts of the Pantjasila with its varied sources continue to be the official philosophy of Indonesia, the at best vaguely defined Personalism of Ngo Dinh Diem is South Vietnam's state philosophy. Personalism seems to represent an amalgam of Catholic social philosophy and Confucianism. Its official statement exalts the "absolute value of the human person," the protection of which is "the sole legitimate end and object of the State" with the proviso that "democracy is neither material happiness nor the supremacy of numbers."

Though Democracy is affirmed throughout Southeast Asia as one of the prime objectives of every regime, like the interpretations of nationalism the content varies widely. In Indonesia, Sukarno seeks for a non-western type of democracy which will replace "the devil of liberalism" with "Guided Democracy . . . the democracy of the family system, without the anarchy of liberalism, without the autocracy of a dictatorship." However lofty the objectives stated of Personalism, there is little question as to the autocracy of Diem's rule in South Vietnam as absolute in its fashion as the party rule in the North. Neither in Thailand nor in Cambodia, for example, does the term have much meaning. In Thailand effective participation in decision-making is confined to a small oligarchy, while in Cambodia the fact that Prince Norodom Sihanouk chooses to have his subjects go through the ritual of elections or plebiscites every so often is interesting but scarcely relevant. In several instances, such as Indonesia, South Vietnam, and Cambodia, the very existence of the state is pinned to the life expectancy of a single individual. Although Ho Chi Minh is demonstrably among Southeast Asia's outstanding figures, the factor of the totalitarian party removes North Vietnam from this category. In the cases of Thailand,

Malaya, and the Philippines, the impersonal factor of the throne in the case of the first two and of the constitution as a focus for national loyalty in the Philippines provide elements of stability. The events of 1958-60 and again in 1962 would seem to indicate that the army is prepared and ready to play a like impersonal role in Burma.

As powerful as are the outside forces influencing the area's ideological development, it seems improbable that, given any sort of free choice, either western liberal democracy or communism as such will triumph. Malaya, the Philippines, and Burma, as of the early sixties, would seem to be the most promising instances of constructive adjustment between foreign ideological influences and indigenous cultural and social inheritance. At the opposite extreme must be placed South Vietnam and Indonesia, with Laos and Cambodia at the mercy of whatever influences predominate in the region.

4. Political Parties and Interest Groups

As in the case of its institutions and ideologies, Southeast Asia presents a picture of bewildering complexity. For the American student, the Philippines offers the most familiar point of departure; for here is an essentially two-party system, distinguished not so much by ideological differences as by the familiar situation of the "Ins," who intend to stay that way, and the "Outs," intent on not staying that way. Familiar also is the fact that the Liberals and the Nationalists within themselves represent loose and shifting coalitions so that, again in typical American fashion, the important policy struggles often take place not between the two parties in election campaigns, but within the victorious party after it has assumed office. In the technical terms used to describe party organization by the French political scientist Maurice Duverger, the Philippine party system, like the American party system, operates on the basis of a caucus-type organization without permanent party bureaucracy, while local activity rests on a foundation of personal relationships. Familiar also to the American student is the existence of recognizable special interest groups, business groups, sugar planters, public-school teachers (reputedly one of the most powerful of pressure groups), the Catholic Church, and the press as a vigilant critic of official corruption and inefficiency. As Magsaysay's success showed, the Philippines increasingly seems to be moving from oligarchic democracy to popular democracy. Given the proper leadership, the average man seems quite capable of deciding for himself without benefit of guidance or control by political oligarchs. The unique American emphasis on the role of the politician as opposed to the administrator seems to have achieved in the independent Philippines the evolution of an increasingly stable and mature democratic political system. The Philippine accomplishment comes closest in Southeast Asia to approximating the stable, secular political systems of more mature democracies.

While Malayan developments have gone far to place that new nation in the same category as the Philippines, there are important reservations to be noted. Clearly, the separate communal basis of political party organization is the only one realistically possible at the present time. To date in Malaya's brief existence as a nation, it has worked well; but as long as the communal divisions continue, the basis of Malaya's political stability remains a fragile one, for it is at the mercy of racial antagonisms or personality conflicts among the leaders of the various communal groups involved. The common British training shared by all, the sheer necessity of cooperation, and the presumably increasing understanding gained by doing so are all potentially hopeful aspects in the Malayan situation. In the American or the Philippine sense, it would seem that pressure groups tend to function within their communal sphere, so that the aggregation and presentation of interests take place within each of the components (Malayan, Chinese, and Indian) of the governing Alliance rather than through lobbying in the legislative or executive branches.

Most alien to both the Philippine and the Malayan political situations is that in North Vietnam, but by the very

nature of its characteristic totalitarian single-party dictatorship, there is an element of familiarity which offers a
basis for understanding. (While it is true that by no means
is there monolithic unity among all the communist parties,
there are sufficient elements in common so that knowledge
of one particular variant aids in understanding another.)
For that matter the all-encompassing but non-totalitarian
nature of Burma's Antifascist Peoples' Freedom League
during the first decade of independence, with its highly
diverse affiliated organizations, bore resemblance to the
Mexican Party of Revolutionary Institutions. As in the
Philippines, the Burmese press seems to function as a
guardian of governmental morality and efficiency. Indeed,
given Burma's one-party hegemony, the press at times
played the critical role that normally would be expected
from a "loyal opposition." Important as interest groups
in the Burmese scene are students, the urban workers, the
Buddhist monks, and the peasants, largely under the leadership of their traditional village officials and of the monks.

During the most recent period of the existence of political parties in Thailand (from the Political Parties Act of
1955 to Field Marshal Sarit's coup of October, 1958),
anyone familiar either with Max Weber's description of
English party organization prior to 1868 as "purely an
organization of notables" or Duverger's characterization of
the same type of group as "a trade union of aspirants for
office" would have found the Thai political scene affording
pertinent case histories. During the periods of their existence, Thai parties seem to have been little more than the
personal following of various contenders for political
power.

Ever since 1932 and particularly since 1947, the armed
forces have consistently played the role of the stern but
kindly guardian of the nation's political destinies, conditioned by the personal ambitions of the senior officers
involved. Other groups, such as the parliamentary politicians, the bureaucracy, the business community, and even
the monarchy itself seem to play roles more as conditioning
rather than as determining factors. As in Indonesia, public

opinion defined as the "newspaper-reading public"—in Thailand estimated at "perhaps no more than 2 per cent of the population," concentrated mostly in Bangkok—is an element which at least has to be taken into consideration in political calculations.

It is at least questionable whether or not Laos and Cambodia should be included in any discussion dealing with political parties and movements. For, grim international implications aside, political history, remote or recent, has presented few spectacles more ludicrous than the Laotian princes sitting around their heavily-laden luncheon table at Geneva and settling the destinies of their nation between mouthfuls of chicken. Apparently it is Laos's unhappy fate to struggle with the terrifying problems of the twentieth century before it has yet relinquished the pre-European fifteenth. Although the creation of the so-called Social Community Party of Cambodia is a tribute to the modern-minded organizational ability of Prince Norodom Sihanouk, it no more belongs in a discussion of political movements than does the retinue of a medieval prince.

In terms of "political anatomy," South Vietnam's party system technically can be classified in the same category as that of Burma prior to the major AFPFL split of April, 1958, for, in both cases, there is a strongly dominant non-totalitarian single party. But there are important distinctions to be noted. In the Kuomintang-like atmosphere of Ngo Dinh Diem's Vietnam, the National Revolutionary Movement, operating both as political party and as a crusade outside and above parties, serves as the officially-approved medium for rallying popular support. Itself under strict control, the Movement receives its chief impetus from the semi-secret, cell-organized Revolutionary Workers' Personalist Party led by Ngo Dinh Nhu. This cadre organization is the "inner party" of the Diem regime. Along with the action taken by government officials, it played a role in the seemingly impressive electoral indorsement given President Diem in April, 1961, when, according to official tabulations, he received 87.8 per cent of the valid votes. It is notable that the Revolutionary Workers' Party attempts to emphasize a leftist role apparently in an effort to meet the Vietminh on its own terms. Aside from his family circle, there is little evidence that public opinion exerts much, if any, influence on President Diem. Public security measures offer little opportunity for either individual or press expressions of opinion. The parallels between the *modus operandi* of the Diem regime in the early sixties and that of Chiang Kai-shek in the late forties appear increasingly ominous for the very survival of South Vietnam as a non-communist let alone democratic state.

Indonesia since March, 1960, has had its political life centered in President Sukarno's National Front, a belated attempt on the President's part to create a universal political movement in his own image. Also appointed in 1960, the present Gotong-Royong (mutual cooperation) unicameral legislature includes representatives of such parties as have not yet been banned by the president and, in approximately equal proportion, spokesmen for various "functional" groups—peasants, labor, youth, armed forces, women's groups, etc. As much as in Vietnam, present and future political developments in Indonesia are all keyed to the life expectancy of one individual. Aside from President Sukarno, there appears to be no other leadership capable of bridging the nation's wide regional and ideological gaps. The two most obvious heirs-apparent, the Army and the Communist Party, were neatly balanced off against each other by the president several years ago. The leadership of neither has shown either the imagination or the ability to make it a logical successor. If in the next few years an aging Sukarno, whose zest for living has been but little curbed by the passage of the years, is no longer on the Indonesian scene, his most likely political heirs are neither the Army nor the Communists but chaos and anarchy.

5. *Social and Cultural Problems*

The variety and complexity of the social and cultural problems faced by contemporary Southeast Asia are such that any attempt to discuss them with the detail they deserve would require a substantial volume; in so brief a survey as this we can only note some of the factors involved. If any one word had to be chosen to characterize and explain the nature of these social and cultural problems perhaps *unevenness* suits best. As we are aware from western political and social history, even when all the varied elements of a society are adjusting to relatively simultaneous pressures at the same time, the transition process can be and usually is one of protracted and unpleasant tension and strain. Think for instance of the agonies experienced by British society in its transitional period of the early nineteenth century. Reflect further that there were decades available to complete this transition, a period of international relaxation of tensions with no problem of national survival involved.

The new nations of Southeast Asia have known all these tensions under the most difficult circumstances. They have been forced to experience them in an era of international tension and turmoil such as the world has never known before. Further, the wrenches and strains of the transition have been neither consistent nor constant. Conditioned by the colonial system and by the particular needs of the particular ruling power, any organic development of the societies as unified wholes was impossible. Some elements were under intensive pressure for rapid change and growth, others were deliberately restrained, and still other aspects of the societies in question simply were left to develop in their own fashion, if at all.

An example of the results produced by these curiously distorted stresses and strains is the development of the city in Southeast Asia. Before the European period there were no cities as such in Southeast Asia. Indeed, the development of cities did not really begin until the period of effective European colonial control in the nineteenth century, and then they developed in a fashion completely different from urban growth in the West. Aside from such artificially created urban centers as Washington or Canberra, modern city growth came about as a development of the age of industrial capitalism. They arose on a solid economic base to meet a concrete need which not only was responsible for bringing them into existence but also insured their future economic and social viability. Southeast Asia's great urban centers, on the other hand, developed not on the basis of indigenous needs and pressures, but as part of the infrastructure created by the colonial powers to service their administrative and commercial needs. The result has been to create in modern Southeast Asia metropolitan areas which in population terms are impressive by anyone's standards* but which lack any real economic justification for their existence or, for that matter, any solid tax base from which to raise the revenues for desperately needed modernization and expansion of municipal facilities.

At the same time, the cities have been the obvious centers of attraction for the uprooted and anomic masses who equate urban existence with the better life. Their fate has been instead to find disillusionment and frustration. It does not seem without significance that it was precisely among this (in the classic Roman sense) proletariat of the bursting metropolitan centers of Java that the Indonesian Communist Party scored striking gains in the elections of the late 1950's. Equally drawn to the cities, especially to the capitals, has been the new generation of the increasingly embittered under-utilized and over-expectant intellectual elite. The result has been to make the cities the center of both political and intellectual activity. In still predominantly agricultural societies, Southeast Asia has predominantly urbanized politics. Yet, in a curiously repetitive fashion, this is a recasting of the familiar and traditional political pattern of court-centered politics far removed from the ken let alone the participation of the peasant masses.

These same masses form one of the major problems of social and cultural change in contemporary Southeast Asia. Until they cease to be masses and become citizens in the twentieth-century sense, meaningful political, economic, or social progress is impossible. All too often we have seen the spectacle of the introduction of the forms of western

* Djakarta almost 3,000,000; Saigon and Manila—2,000,000; Singapore—1,300,000.

governmental processes with the role of the masses reduced to little more than that of passive and regimented participants. To introduce the structure of advanced government uprooted from the social and cultural environment in which it has evolved is to shade the odds yet further against the prospects of success. Obviously very closely connected with the political aspect of the whole problem of modernization is the question: how in the social and cultural sense to convert these masses into twentieth-century citizens. The need for coherent progress is obvious; the way to achieve it is something else again.

Nor, in many cases, have the ruling elite shown any notable capacity to solve the problems involved. It has been a curious irony, most tragically demonstrated in the case of Indonesia, that the ability to provide brilliant leadership during the independence struggle frequently bears little or no relation to the talents required to govern. For obvious reasons, important sections of the ruling elite have little enthusiasm for social and economic reforms calculated to destroy their particular worlds; the conflict that has developed between generations in this connection is not surprising. As the numbers of those who by birth or education feel themselves to be at least candidate members of the ruling elite have increased, the possibilities for rapid upper mobility such as the revolutionary generation possessed have become increasingly less and their frustration increasingly greater. Involved in this would seem to be both personal career considerations and a conviction of greater competence. It is significant that, throughout the Asian-African world in recent years, the armed forces, predominantly the officers corps of the army, have been the chief source of vigorous efforts to achieve governmental reform by the introduction of new concepts of both rationalized and honest administration. Whether, as in the cases of Burma and Thailand, these various army coups have been led by senior officers or, as in the abortive army coups in Laos and South Vietnam, by officers of junior rank, the officer corps has represented the only organized group both

able to take action and acutely aware of the need to do so.*
Power once achieved, the ability to cope successfully with
the problems involved is, of course, another matter.

Agrarian reform, social welfare, internal security, population pressures, a rationalized bureaucracy, illiteracy,
encouragement of the development of an occupationally
balanced middle class, consciousness of nationhood, development of internal social integration, peaceful transfer of
political power, meaningful involvement of the masses in
the political process, creation of more balanced economies
—all these have bearing on the wrenching processes of
social and cultural adjustment to the modern world which
contemporary Southeast Asia is presently undergoing.

The fact that the process has begun is in itself no guarantee that it will be completed; the possibilities of complete
or partial failure are always there. Above all is the ominous
time factor. If these transitions are to be accomplished by
non-totalitarian means, they must show substantial progress
within the next few years. And even that substantial progress must pack within those few years the achievements
that Western Europe needed decades to accomplish. This
accomplishment, it would seem clear, is beyond the unaided
powers of any of the new Southeast Asian nations. Like it
or not, the West cannot allow these new nations to turn to
the communist bloc simply by default. Nor is foreign aid
important merely in its own right. As has been demonstrated many times, it brings with it important social and
cultural influences.

6. *Economic Problems and Foreign Aid*

If any one set of problems can be said to be paramount,
it is the economic. Unless there are solid economic foun-

* The role of the military in the emerging nations as dynamic
forces for modernization has long been a significant one. The
part played by the samurai in Japan has often been cited. Less
well known is the fact that the events which brought about
British occupation of Egypt in 1882 were initiated by an unsuccessful revolt in 1881 of western-oriented, junior-grade army
officers against the corrupt and archaic Khedival regime.

dations, few of the others can even be hopefully attacked let alone solved. Foreign aid in itself is no answer. Foreign aid as a catalyst for transforming the static agricultural economies from their passive states of little or no growth is a requisite. In none of the new nations is there either sufficient domestic capital or entrepreneurial skill to achieve unaided the "take-off" for self-sustaining economic growth. Pressing heavily on all the new governments is the need to make at least a start towards redeeming those promissory notes on the future which the social and economic sections of their constitutions so often embody. Equally pressing is the desperate and, in most cases to date, the losing race to achieve economic growth in the face of consistently mounting population pressure on already inadequate resources.* As in the case of Lewis Carroll's Alice, before any actual progress can be registered, it is necessary to run faster and faster merely to stay in the same place.

The creation of balanced economies to escape from the uneasy dependence on the fluctuating income from one or two agricultural or extractive export commodities is an obvious must. But this calls not only for industrial but also for agricultural development. To attempt to develop an industrial economy while leaving the traditional agricultural sphere unchanged would be to invite both economic and social disaster; the creation of an industrial economy requires the most careful planning. In this connection there seems to have developed an increasing sense of realism. Rather early in the '50's it became clear that however desirable a national status symbol the possession of a steel industry may be, it is folly to try to create it at impossible cost when neither the natural resources available nor the potential market justify the project. Also complicating industrial development is the obvious fact that technicians and skilled workers cannot be trained overnight. Handicapping the problem of agricultural rationalization is the traditional conservatism of the peasant masses and the

* Demographers project a population increase for Southeast Asia between now and the year 2000 to approximately 300,000,-000 from the present estimated 200,000,000.

chronic difficulties of communication between them and the governing elite.

Availability of unlimited funds offers no magic guarantee of success in itself. Indeed, as the sordid history of Kuomintang China in the postwar period demonstrates, it can be a potent force for disaster. Nor is the record in either Laos or South Vietnam calculated to offer much encouragement. Since the mid-50's the United States and the Soviet Union have engaged in a deadly serious competition to win the favor of the new nations through lavish aid programs. The previously cited instance of Cambodia is an almost classic illustration of the fashion in which the smallest and weakest of neutral nations can use this competition as a type of diplomatic judo to make the most powerful nations gratify its whims for conspicuous symbols of modernization without any particular reference to their real appropriateness for the country.

More seems likely to be accomplished in terms of constructive rather than of competitive aid programs if the assistance were channeled through some such agency as the Colombo Plan or the United Nations. It is notable that the Colombo Plan, initiated in 1950 without any actual funds of its own and as a Commonwealth Project, is the one aid program in which all of the Southeast Asian nations, North Vietnam excepted, participate. The Colombo Plan itself, or an organization modelled on it, seems best calculated to meet the psychological objections and suspicions which both Soviet and American programs cause.

In terms of economic development it is only realistic to accept the fact that governmental control and planning will continue to be permanent factors in the Southeast Asian scheme, although rather less so perhaps than would have been predicted a decade ago. It is notable, for example, that so previously dedicated and doctrinaire a democratic socialist as U Nu, in one of his first public statements after resuming the premiership in April, 1960, announced not only that there would be no more nationalization of private enterprises but that those incapable of efficient state operation would be returned to private hands. Not surprisingly,

Malaya, although it too has a second Five Year Plan projected for 1961-1965, from the beginning of its independent existence has taken steps to attract diversified foreign capital investment through favorable tax and other exemptions.

At the opposite ideological pole, among the non-communist nations, the Philippines, although officially dedicated to free enterprise concepts, initiated in 1957 a five-year plan calling for a higher degree of government investment. For although the Philippines has available sources for domestic capital investment, those controlling them have shown little of that frugal puritan spirit, with its willingness to tie up its funds in long-range capital investment, which was so important a factor in the English or the Japanese industrialization process. The economic problems confronting the Philippines are the familiar ones of achieving a balanced economy with an anticipated rise in living standards.

In common with the Philippines, South Vietnam faces both the necessity for agrarian reform and the shortage of domestic capital. Unlike the Philippines or Malaya, Vietnam can offer little inducement for foreign investment, with the result that extensive American subsidy, motivated by obvious geopolitical considerations, must continue indefinitely. The continuing reliance on rice and rubber production as the nation's only important exports underlines the vulnerability of Vietnam's economy. Add to this the factors of the inescapable necessity of expenditures for refugee resettlement, a disproportionately large military force which cannot be reduced, and highly inefficient and corrupt revenue collection. The sum total is not calculated to inspire optimism about Vietnam's economic future let alone any expectations of progressive change.

Although not confronted with the pressing and perilous challenges which are South Vietnam's lot, Indonesia's economic future in the early 1960's seems equally clouded. Potentially Southeast Asia's richest nation, with rubber and oil exports the country's chief foreign-exchange earners, chronic inflation, diversion of revenues by the consistently semi-rebellious military regimes of the other islands, and official mismanagement of economic affairs have all contributed to Indonesia's condition of perennial economic crisis. Constitutionally dedicated from its beginnings as an independent nation to achievement of a socialist type of managed economy, Indonesia in 1961 launched a grandiose eight-year program for the development of "Indonesian socialism" which was to represent a blending of the indigenous communal traditions with modern planning. Although between 1955 and 1960 Indonesia received approximately $250,000,000 in economic aid from the U.S. plus almost $500,000,000 from the Soviet Union, there was little of a constructive nature to show for it. With poorer prospects for improvement and less justification than other nations of Southeast Asia, Indonesia faced the 1960's with all of the characteristic economic problems not only unsolved but intensified.

Although, like the rest of Southeast Asia, depending primarily on a single important export crop (rice), Thailand in the early 1960's seemed to be not only the most socially content but the most economically sound country of the area. There was neither an official economic plan nor apparently any particular pressure for one. And at the end of the fifties, a World Bank report termed the nation's economy "active and growing" with its finances and currency "in a strong and sound condition." Through tax incentives the government was attempting to offer inducements for foreign capital investment to achieve industrial development. Operating as the nation does without urgent pressures of either strongly dissatisfied economic groups or the threat of population growth on food resources, it seemed unlikely that Thailand's economic position would experience any substantial change in the coming decade.

7. *Minorities and Regionalism*

Leaving the Chinese question for later discussion, only Burma and Indonesia have minority problems of any importance. Burma's problems have both racial and regional aspects while Indonesia's are primarily regional. It seems clear that the wounds of the desperate struggle to keep

Burma together as a political entity are far from healed, with any feeling of common national unity yet to be achieved. In 1960 the right of the chiefs of the important Shan minority to have separate representation in the Chamber of Nationalities was abolished by legislative action. While it seems unlikely that either the Shan or the Karen minorities will again engage in armed revolt, both seem determined to guard jealously the privileges of their separate states and to resist any process of Burmanization. To date the smaller Arakanese and Mon minorities have not yet achieved their goals of similar states. All these groups both culturally and religiously seem likely to remain people apart from the dominant Burmese majority for some time to come.

Indonesia's minority problems are less those of the traditional antagonism of the other peoples of the archipelago against the Javanese and more the bitterness of the outer islands brought about by the central government's indifference to their problems. The decade of the fifties saw various areas in the Outer Islands, under Army leadership, repeatedly initiate policies of virtual economic secession from Djakarta, with such valuable exports as copra and rubber "smuggled" out of the country under local Army protection and the revenues then retained by the region involved for local needs. Although federalism is tainted with the memories of the use made of it by the Dutch during the revolutionary period, it seems that sooner or later some variety of it offers the only solution to Indonesia's crucial problem of regionalism. To date the central government has yet to meet the well justified demands for both administrative autonomy and a just share of the revenues produced by the Outer Islands. Until that time comes, regionalism will remain one of Indonesia's most pressing internal problems.

Uniquely in Burma do the Chinese enjoy the experience of not being the envied and suspect minority as a result of their superior and often too sharp business acumen. For in Burma, the Indian money-lending castes who flocked in during the British period and profited from peasant financial naïveté are cast in this unenviable role which the Chinese play elsewhere. In Thailand, for example, the Chinese form the only substantial minority group, somewhat over 11 per cent of the entire population. But, as with everything else in Thailand, the Chinese problem is apparently not a critical one. There seems to be no evidence that the Chinese community has ever united to exercise its considerable economic power; the basic question seems to be one of long-range social and political assimilation. With fresh immigration severely restricted in recent years, and with unenthusiastic but correct relations maintained with the Nationalist regime, the possibilities for overt intervention by either China have been kept to a minimum. This coupled with the recent efforts by the Thai government to carry out an assimilation policy and with the lack of popular antagonism towards the Chinese minority would seem to augur well for the future.

In Indonesia, the Chinese ever since independence have been paying the price for their longtime economic alliance with the Dutch in the same fashion that the politically and economically impotent Eurasian minority has had to pay the price for its role during the colonial period. The closest analogy to the Chinese position during the last fifteen years is that endured by the Jews in medieval Europe. For the Chinese, too, have made a highly important economic contribution to the nation's economy with their virtual monopoly of commercial trade, and they too have incurred hostility and suspicion as a result not only of this but also by their dogged dedication to their own traditional manners and mores. For generations they have defied both racial and cultural assimilation and obviously intend to continue doing so.

The fact that it is Peking rather than Taiwan with which Djakarta maintains diplomatic relations does not greatly aid the approximate 2,500,000 Chinese minority. As economic and social pressures mounted in Indonesia during the 1950's, the Chinese increasingly were cast in a traditional scapegoat role. At first measures, usually decrees by regional military commanders, singled out Kuomintang supporters, both because of their lack of any powerful foreign protector and also because of the resentment aroused by the support given the Sumatran and Celebes 1958 revolt by the Nationalist Chinese. But in 1959 a governmental decree was announced, and implemented in January, 1960, which banned "foreign traders" from engaging in business anywhere except in certain designated metropolitan areas. In spite of Peking's angry protests, the Army pushed it through not only to the misery of the Chinese community but to the serious harm of the Indonesian economy. In the early 1960's Indonesia's Chinese minority remained as unassimilated as ever and probably far more ready to act as Peking's fifth column than had been the case before.

Next to Indonesia, South Vietnam has pursued perhaps the most harsh policy towards its Chinese minority. Here there is not only the familiar economic hostility but the traditional memories of the long periods of Chinese imperial domination to which the occupation of the north by Kuomintang troops after World War II added a bitter and unpleasant chapter. Today as traditionally, Chinese imperialism continues to be the chief peril to the existence of an independent Vietnam. As in the case of Indonesia, the Saigon government has taken restrictive political and economic measures against its substantial (somewhat over 6 per cent) Chinese minority without apparently having been able to force any solutions. A state of unresolved tension seems to characterize Vietnam's Chinese problem in the early sixties. While any assessment of the political sentiments of the Chinese community is impossible, it seems logical to conclude that their feelings towards the Diem regime are anything but sympathetic. To a less vehement extent, the Philippine Chinese minority (slightly over 1 per cent) has experienced the same tribulations as those of Indonesia and South Vietnam. Only in Malaya, through sheer weight of numbers and the happy circumstance of enlightened leadership on both sides, does there presently seem to be a real prospect of the Chinese community becoming an integrated part of a functioning and viable communal society.

8. The Foreign Relations of Southeast Asia

The major foreign affairs problem confronting the new nations of Southeast Asia is exactly the same as that with which Thailand has for so long and so skillfully struggled, i.e., sheer survival. The varying responses to this challenge serve to demonstrate that there is no common regional outlook. The various responses range from the outright adherence of North Vietnam to the communist bloc to the membership of Thailand and the Philippines in the anti-communist Southeast Asia Treaty Organization (SEATO), brought into existence after the unhappy Geneva conference by U.S. Secretary of State John Foster Dulles as part of his comprehensive containment project. The Philippines' allegiance to the anticommunist world is not subject to question. As the 1960's began, continued communist advances in Laos and South Vietnam offered a growing threat to Thailand's security. Lacking the geographical isolation of the Philippines, it was clear that Thailand's subversion would represent the next major target if communist efforts were successful in Laos and South Vietnam. For a people possessed of such an acute sense of political survival as the Thai, there was every reason to consider at least the possibility that the east wind would prevail and what the consequences would be for Thailand. Embroiled in quarrels with its traditional enemies, Vietnam and Thailand, Cambodia's future seemed even more dubious.

Although avoiding commitment to SEATO, the cornerstone of Malaya's foreign policy rests on a defense and mutual assistance treaty with Great Britain. It seems proper to rate Malaya, along with the Philippines, as one of the most pro-western of the Southeast Asian nations. Its relations with its giant "brother" nation of Indonesia are characterized by wary friendliness. Among certain groups both in Malaya and Indonesia there are dreams of a political union which revive the glories of the ancient Malaysian empires at their maximum extent. For the foreseeable future, however, for Malaya there is obviously little to be gained and much to be lost in any very close association with Indonesia. Barring a western debacle in Southeast Asia, an orientation towards Great Britain and the Commonwealth seems likely to characterize Malaya's foreign policy for some time to come.

While understandably uneasy over Peking's long-range intentions, Burma has never abandoned its policy of neutrality and non-alignment with either of the major power blocs. Although originally, as is still the case with others among the Asian and African nations, Burmese leadership tended to forgive the Soviet Union and condemn the United States in advance on world issues, the sobering responsibilities and experiences of the past decade seem to have brought about a far more neutrally neutral outlook. Indeed the fact that both the United States and the Soviet Union regarded Burma as truly neutral was indicated by their joint support in November, 1961, of a Burmese diplomat (U Thant) to become acting Secretary-General of the United Nations and thus end the crisis created by the tragic death of Dag Hammarskjold.

Like Burma, Indonesia throughout its national existence has been officially committed to what is termed "an independent but active foreign policy." During recent years it has often seemed that this policy was far less truly neutral towards the communist world than towards the West. Indeed Indonesia's attitude has often seemed to be that of a friendly willingness to accept any statements emanating from Moscow, if not always Peking, at rather more than par value, while American policy utterances are subjected to wary and suspicious scrutiny. Particularly in connection with that prime issue of national prestige, the "Irian" (West New Guinea) issue, Moscow and Peking have always been lavish in their expressions of moral support and sympathy while the western powers, above all the United States, have found themselves impaled on the horns of that familiar dilemma of competing policy requirements in Europe and Asia. That the Soviet Union at least is now ready to give rather more than moral support on the Irian issue seemed indicated when Indonesian Chief of Staff Major-General Nasution signed a military agreement in Moscow in January, 1961, for the delivery of a reported $400,000,000 worth of aircraft, submarines and torpedo boats which would result, the General later told Indonesian correspondents, in the doubling of Indonesia's military strength.

On a regional basis there has never existed any sort of Southeast Asian bloc or league. Adherence, with varying degrees of either consistency or enthusiasm, to that broad, shifting, and feud-split grouping of the United Nations known as the Asian-African bloc has represented to date the maximum degree of geographical grouping which the nations of the area have been able to achieve since their independence. The much-publicized Bandung (Indonesia) conference of April, 1955, which brought together the leaders of the Afro-Asian world in an exclusive meeting for the first time in history, resulted in little more than a series of vaguely-worded resolutions favoring world peace, economic and cultural cooperation, and condemning western colonialism. The then Prime Minister of Ceylon (Sir John Kotelawala) received strong criticism from many fellow delegates for venturing to refer to "Soviet imperialism" as equally deserving of condemnation. The trend of world affairs in the years since the Bandung Conference offers unhappy testimony as to its meagre results. Although from time to time trial balloons for the convening of a new Bandung conference are launched, particularly from Indonesian sources,* the proposals seem to have aroused but slight enthusiasm among either those nations in attendance at the first conference or the considerable group which have achieved sovereignty since 1955.

* In March, 1961, for example, it was reported that President Sukarno had despatched a "roving ambassador" to sound out Asian-African opinion on the possibility of convening a second Bandung conference to consider means of easing international tensions.

Perhaps the most realistic and potentially hopeful of regional developments, uniquely, completely Southeast Asian in inspiration, was the announcement after a conference in Bangkok in late July, 1961, that Thailand, Malaya, and the Philippines were joining together to launch an Association of Southeast Asian states (ASA) which, among the non-communist nations of the area, was intended "to promote mutual assistance in economic, social, cultural, scientific and administrative fields." There was even hopeful talk by the sponsoring powers of the eventual creation of a Southeast Asian common market which would aid in seeking "stable world prices for Southeast Asia's rubber, tin, copra, etc." Although Indonesia remained aloof, the new grouping possesses a considerable potential, time and circumstances permitting. As the *New York Times* (August 8) commented editorially just after the announcement of its formation, "If the proposed Malaysian Commonwealth welding Malaya, Singapore, Sarawak, Brunei, and North Borneo into a new federation materializes as a member, the ASA would represent more than fifty million people and be of real consequence in world affairs."

The immediate postwar period in Southeast Asia presented an opportunity for the United States to play a dynamic role unique in history. As the world's unchallengeable military and economic power in those immediate postwar years, the United States could have required and enforced an acceptance by the European powers of the fact that the colonial era had ended. A bold and imaginative assertion of the American belief in the self-determination of peoples and the rights of man should have been made; the results might well have changed the whole course of postwar history, especially in terms of the relations between the western world and the new nations of Asia and Africa. Under American auspices a peaceful and orderly transition to independence could have taken place. Neither France nor the Netherlands would have experienced the futile bitterness of long years of colonial war with their pointless waste of lives and resources and the subsequent harvest of hate and alienation. Instead, perhaps under United Nations auspices, an international Southeast Asian development authority might have opened new vistas for creative cooperation between the former colonial powers and the new nations at a fraction of the cost involved in futile colonial wars and efforts to "contain" the spread of communism.

Had the United States taken such steps, world communism would have been deprived of the opportunity to pose as a liberating force or as the sponsor of movements for independence from colonial rule.. It was not without significance that the first British troops to reach Java after the Japanese surrender found quotations from Lincoln's Gettysburg Address, rather than from the Communist Manifesto, chalked on the walls of buildings by the Indonesian nationalists. Particularly in the period between the Japanese surrender and the outbreak of colonial wars in Indo-China and Java, there was present the opportunity for bold and imaginative leadership.

By 1962 all this had changed. Except in reproach or mockery, the Gettysburg Address and the Declaration of Independence were no longer quoted, and the image of the United States was that of the automatic supporter of any status quo regime as long as it was status quo and sufficiently vehemently anticommunist in its public statements. By sheer default the United States had surrendered the moral and psychological initiative in Southeast Asia to the communist world. Whether a second opportunity like that of 1945-1946 will present itself seems dubious at best.

Should the horror of thermo-nuclear war explode upon the world in the decade of the sixties, then the fate of Southeast Asia as of the rest of the world is beyond meaningful speculation. If, however, the present stalemate of terror continues, the very delicacy of the balance between the opposing forces may give the nations of Southeast Asia a unique opportunity to work out their own destinies. To do this with any degree of success, both extensive economic aid and the development of a new and competent leadership will be necessary. In terms of patience, understanding, and sympathetic assistance, given without patronage or formal obligations, this might well be a possibility for the United States to create, if not so bold, at least as constructive a role for itself as it could have in the late 1940's. Whether this, coupled with similar policies elsewhere in the other developing areas of the world, could actually make an effective contribution to the reduction of world tensions is problematical. But the challenge is there. If it is accepted in terms of a basic dedication to the peace and stability of the world rather than in terms of the Cold War or geopolitical strategy, the results might well be encouraging not only for the stabilization and progressive development of Southeast Asia but for their impact on international affairs generally.

SUGGESTED READINGS

(This is not intended as a list for the specialist with access to the resources of an academic library but rather for the intelligent general reader. To this end, an effort has been made to keep the list reasonably brief and also to include paperback sources.) In terms of periodical coverage most easily available to the general reader, *The New York Times* and *The Christian Science Monitor* are probably the most outstanding and also nationally circulated. Among magazines giving particular attention to Asian affairs, in terms of political rather than historical emphasis, *Pacific Affairs* is outstanding. Since, however, it is available only by subscription, *The Reporter* and *Foreign Affairs* are more likely to be most available in any local library.

General Works: (Those marked with an asterisk while not primarily concerned with Southeast Asia are nevertheless valuable in terms of background coverage.)

Adloff, Virginia, and Thompson, Richard, *Minority Problems in Southeast Asia.* Stanford: Stanford University Press, 1955. Somewhat dated but standard.

Dean, Vera M., *The Nature of the Non-Western World.* New York: The New American Library, Mentor Series, 1957 (paperback). An excellent general introduction to the general problems involved with separate sections on each area.

Dobby, E. H. G., *South East Asia.* 6th ed., London: University of London Press, 1958. The standard geographical work exclusively devoted to the area.

DuBois, Cora, *Social Forces in Southeast Asia.* Cambridge:

Harvard University Press, 1959. A reprint of a brilliant series of lectures initially delivered in 1949 but timeless.

Elsbree, Willard H., *Japan's Role in Southeast Asian Nationalist Movements.* Cambridge: Harvard University Press, 1953.

* Emerson, Rupert, *From Empire to Nation: The Rise to Self-Assertion of Asian and African Peoples.* Cambridge: Harvard University Press, 1960. This most recent work by a distinguished scholar is probably destined to become the standard source on the development of non-western nationalism.

Fifeld, Russell H., *The Diplomacy of Southeast Asia, 1945-1958.* New York: Harper, 1958. An impressive and comprehensive pioneering work.

Furnivall, J. S., *Colonial Policy and Practice: A Comparative Study of Burma and Netherlands India.* New York: New York University Press, 1956. A reissue of a classic study by a distinguished scholar-administrator.

Harrison, Brian, *A Short History of South-East Asia.* New York: St. Martin's Press, 1954. Scholarly, well-written and brief—probably the best historical introduction available for the non-specialist.

* Johnson, John J., *The Role of the Military in Underdeveloped Countries.* Princeton: Princeton University Press, 1962.

Kahin, George McT. (editor), *Governments and Politics of Southeast Asia.* Ithaca: Cornell University Press, 1959. The definitive text and likely to remain so.

Lensen, George A., *The World Beyond Europe.* Cambridge: Houghton-Mifflin, 1960 (paperback). Highly recommended as an introduction, painless but authoritative, to the history of the non-western world.

Millikan, Max F., and Blackmer, Donald L. M., *The Emerging Nations, Their Growth and United States Policy.* Boston: Little, Brown & Co., 1961 (paperback). An authoritative and highly successful "exercise in interdisciplinary analysis."

Pye, Lucian W., "The Politics of Southeast Asia," in Almond, Gabriel A., and Coleman, James S. (editors), *The Politics of the Developing Areas.* Princeton: Princeton University Press, 1960. Probably destined to become the standard text but the high price ($10.00) is likely to give pause except for the interested specialist. The student of the methodology of comparative politics will find the initial and concluding sections of particular interest.

Trager, Frank N. (editor), *Marxism in Southeast Asia.* Stanford: Stanford University Press, 1959. More for the specialist than for the general reader but of value.

Vandenbosch, Amry, and Butwell, Richard, *Southeast Asia Among the World Powers.* Lexington: University of Kentucky Press, 1957. Judicious and well-balanced. See also the just-published *Southeast Asia Today—And Tomorrow: A Political Analysis* by Richard Butwell. New York: Frederick A. Praeger, 1961 (paperback).

Burma:

Cady, John F., *A History of Modern Burma.* Ithaca: Cornell University Press, 1958.

Maung Maung, *Burma's Constitution.* The Hague: Martinus Nijhoff, 1959.

Tinker, Hugh. *The Union of Burma.* 2nd ed., London and New York: Oxford University Press, 1959.

Cambodia:

Herz, Martin F., *A Short History of Cambodia.* New York: Praeger, 1958.

Steinberg, David (editor), *Cambodia: Its People, Its Society, Its Culture.* Human Relations Area Files. New York: Taplinger Publishing Co., 1959.

Indonesia:

Hanna, Willard A., *Bung Karno's Indonesia.* Rev. Ed., New York: American Universities Field Staff, 1961.

Kahin, George McT., *Nationalism and Revolution in Indonesia.* Ithaca: Cornell University Press, 1952.

Vlekke, Bernard H. M., *Nusantara: A History of Indonesia.* Rev. Ed., Chicago: Quadrangle, 1959.

Laos:

Fall, Bernard B., *Laos, Background of a Conflict.* Washington: Public Affairs Press, 1961.

LeBar, Frank M. (editor), *Laos: Its People, Its Society, Its Culture.* Human Relations Area Files. New York: Taplinger Publishing Co., 1960.

Sisouk Na Champassak, *Storm Over Laos: A Contemporary History.* New York: Praeger, 1961.

Malaya:

Ginsburg, Norton, and Roberts, Chester F., Jr., *Malaya.* Human Relations Area Files. Seattle: University of Washington Press, 1958.

Parkinson, C. Northcote, *A Short History of Malaya.* Singapore: Donald Moore, 1954.

Winstedt, Sir Richard C., *The Malays, A Cultural History.* Rev. Ed., London: Routledge & Kegan Paul, Ltd., 1950.

The Philippines:

Bernstein, David, *The Philippine Story*. New York: Farrar, Straus & Cudahy, 1947.

Hayden, Joseph R., *The Philippines: A Study in National Development*. New York: The Macmillan Co., 1942.

Smith, Robert A., *Philippine Freedom, 1946-1958*. New York: Columbia University Press, 1958.

Thailand:

Blanchard, Wendell, and others, *Thailand: Its People, Its Society, Its Culture*. Human Relations Area Files. New York: Taplinger Publishing Company, 1958.

Coast, John, *Some Aspects of Thai Politics*. New York: Institute of Pacific Relations, 1953.

Vella, Walter, *The Impact of the West on Government in Thailand*. Berkeley: University of California Press, 1955.

Vietnam, North:

Fall, Bernard B., *The Viet-Minh Regime: Government and Administration in the Democratic Republic of Vietnam*. 2nd ed., New York: Institute of Pacific Relations, 1956.

Vietnam, South:

Hammer, Ellen, *The Struggle for Indochina*. Stanford: Stanford University Press, 1954.

———, *The Struggle for Indochina Continues*. Stanford: Stanford University Press, 1955.

Lindholm, Richard W. (editor), *Viet-Nam: The First Five Years*. East Lansing: Michigan State University Press, 1959.